UNIQUELY URBAN
CASE STUDIES IN INNOVATIVE URBAN DEVELOPMENT

FEBRUARY 2023

ASIAN DEVELOPMENT BANK

 Creative Commons Attribution 3.0 IGO license (CC BY 3.0 IGO)

© 2023 Asian Development Bank
6 ADB Avenue, Mandaluyong City, 1550 Metro Manila, Philippines
Tel +63 2 8632 4444; Fax +63 2 8636 2444
www.adb.org

Some rights reserved. Published in 2023.

ISBN 978-92-9269-966-6 (print), 978-92-9269-967-3 (electronic); 978-92-9269-968-0 (ebook)
Publication Stock No. TCS220583-2
DOI: http://dx.doi.org/10.22617/TCS220583-2

The views expressed in this publication are those of the authors and do not necessarily reflect the views and policies of the Asian Development Bank (ADB) or its Board of Governors or the governments they represent.

ADB does not guarantee the accuracy of the data included in this publication and accepts no responsibility for any consequence of their use. The mention of specific companies or products of manufacturers does not imply that they are endorsed or recommended by ADB in preference to others of a similar nature that are not mentioned.

By making any designation of or reference to a particular territory or geographic area, or by using the term "country" in this document, ADB does not intend to make any judgments as to the legal or other status of any territory or area.

This work is available under the Creative Commons Attribution 3.0 IGO license (CC BY 3.0 IGO) https://creativecommons.org/licenses/by/3.0/igo/. By using the content of this publication, you agree to be bound by the terms of this license. For attribution, translations, adaptations, and permissions, please read the provisions and terms of use at https://www.adb.org/terms-use#openaccess.

This CC license does not apply to non-ADB copyright materials in this publication. If the material is attributed to another source, please contact the copyright owner or publisher of that source for permission to reproduce it. ADB cannot be held liable for any claims that arise as a result of your use of the material.

Please contact pubsmarketing@adb.org if you have questions or comments with respect to content, or if you wish to obtain copyright permission for your intended use that does not fall within these terms, or for permission to use the ADB logo.

Corrigenda to ADB publications may be found at http://www.adb.org/publications/corrigenda.

Note:
In this publication, "$" refers to United States dollars.
ADB recognizes "China" as the People's Republic of China.

On the cover: *Uniquely Urban* is the consolidation of Asian Development Bank's urban development case studies to introduce innovative thinkers, ideas, and projects.

Cover design by Nonie Villanueva.

Contents

Figures and Boxes	vi
Foreword	vii
Acknowledgments	viii
Abbreviations	x
Introduction	1

1	How Upstream Programmatic Interventions Drive Industrial and Urban Transformation	7
2	How People-Friendly Urban Mobility and Green Sponge Infrastructure is Transforming a City	17
3	A First in Viet Nam's Water Sector: Utility Transitions to Nonsovereign Lending	31
4	Nonsovereign PRC Loan Demonstrates Broad Integration of Smart Water Technologies	41
5	Beyond Slum Upgrades: How Affordable Housing Projects Build Resilient, Thriving Households	49
6	ADB's First Blue Loan Intercepts Plastics from Landfills, Oceans through Recycling, and Reuse of Ubiquitous PET	61
7	Private Sector Team in Georgia Expands Green Bond Market in Asia, Urban Water Sector	69
8	Integrating Urban Design, Nature, and Heritage for Tourism in a Cold-Climate Country: Preliminary ADB Lessons from Mongolia	75
9	The Making of a Market-Based Mortgage Sector	85

Figures and Boxes

Figures

1	Transport Corridor Versus Industrial Corridor	9
2	The Visakhapatnam–Chennai Industrial Corridor	10
3	Overall Concept Plan of the Project	19
4	Illustration of Rapid Bus Transit Station	20
5	Illustrations of Sponge City Green Infrastructure Planning and Examples	22
6	Visual Aid of Flash Points to be Managed based on Hydraulic Modeling	25
7	Visual Summary of Sponge City Green Infrastructure Master Plan	26
8	Water Distress in the People's Republic of China	42
9	The Scale of Tamil Nadu's Housing Shortage	51
10	The Problem with Plastics	63
11	Map of Mongolia Phase 1 and Phase 2 Project Areas	80

Boxes

1	Summary of Intended Results for the India Visakhapatnam–Chennai Industrial Corridor Development Program	13
2	Summary of Intended Results for the Jilin Yanji Low Carbon Climate Resilient Healthy City Project	26
3	Summary of Intended Results for Viet Nam: The Binh Duong Water Treatment Expansion Project	37
4	Sponge City and Smart Water Defined	43
5	Summary of Intended Results for the Climate Resilient and Smart Urban Water Infrastructure Project in the People's Republic of China	46
6	Summary of Intended Results	58
7	Summary of Intended Results for the Georgia Green Bond Project	73
8	Summary of Intended Results for the Uzbekistan: Mortgage Market Sector Development Program	91

Foreword

We are proud to publish *Uniquely Urban*, a set of case studies on innovative project designs to inform thinking and approaches to making cities more livable in the Asia and Pacific region. As the region rebuilds better and stronger from the Coronovirus disease (COVID-19) pandemic, innovations will be the key to maintaining equitable, sustainable, and resilient growth.

In ADB, innovation is the cornerstone of our operations. For us, innovation is a coveted pool of energy, which fosters higher efficiencies, delivers greater development impacts from smaller ecological footprints, and achieves more effective and equitable distribution of opportunities and benefits. Innovation may be a truly novel solution to an old problem, a slight variation to a mode of project implementation, or the creation of an entire new development ecosystem. It may simply be the transfer of technology, knowledge, and capacity from where it is standard to where it is new.

Innovations across ADB are well represented in this collection of case studies. *Uniquely Urban* features innovations across sectors, thematic areas and subregions, and nearly all are in emerging investment areas. These include healthy and age-friendly cities, affordable housing, sustainable tourism and heritage conservation, circular economy and ocean health, low carbon development, inclusive urban mobility, economic corridor development, and resilient cities.

Innovative financing is a common feature of the case studies, such as ADB's first Blue Loan that will redirect plastics from oceans and landfills, the expansion of nonsovereign lending to a traditional sector such as water supply, and the strengthening of markets for green bonds. Many of the firsts for developing member countries (DMCs) are also the firsts for ADB, a testament to our trusted partnerships and our ability to translate concepts into actions and benefits.

ADB's Urban Sector Group made many of these innovations possible by convening multi-disciplinary experts from across our operational landscape and DMCs to determine the best solutions to the challenging problems. By using bold and diverse approaches, project officers and the partners from DMCs are seeing substantial development impacts.

The Urban Sector Group has demonstrated thought leadership in proactively sharing the experiences of our operations teams, promoting creative thinking, and maximizing development outcomes. I congratulate Manoj Sharma, the chief of the urban sector group and his team, the ADB staff whose projects are featured here, and our DMC partners who designed and implemented these innovative solutions. I would encourage our ADB teams to regularly document and share such impactful developments.

Woochong Um
Managing Director General
Asian Development Bank

Acknowledgments

This report was commissioned by ADB management to document innovation in the design of urban projects. It aims to provide valuable guidance on livable cities to ADB's project officers and DMC partners, offering novel knowledge solutions that address the complex and challenging problems facing the Asia and Pacific region. The case studies attest to the value of multi-disciplinary teams and the One ADB approach, the perseverance that innovation sometimes requires, and the multiple benefits to sectors, countries, and regions when innovation succeeds in delivering new financing modes and new design approaches.

Manoj Sharma, chief of the urban sector group, and Hong Soo Lee, senior urban specialist (Smart Cities) in the Sustainable Development and Climate Change Department (SDCC) of the Asian Development Bank led the overall preparation of this publication and provided technical guidance. Consultant Melissa Alipalo led the interviews with project staff, drafted the case studies in consultation with the project officers, and managed the editorial production process. Lindy Lois Gamolo, senior operations assistant, and Aldrin Plaza, senior project officer in the Urban Sector Group of SDCC, provided valuable administrative and technical support to the team.

For their endorsement, support, and guidance in this knowledge initiative, the team wishes to acknowledge the SDCC Director General Bruno Carrasco, SDCC officer Sungsup Ra, and the Urban Sector Group Committee.

The case studies offer additional value to readily available project documents because of the personal engagement and collaboration of the following case study project staff: Peter Marro and Bobir Baisovich Gafurov of the Mortgage Market Sector Development Program in Uzbekistan.

Manoj Sharma, Akira Matsunaga, Pushkar Srivastava, and Ashwin Hosur Viswanath of the Visakhapatnam-Chennai Industrial Corridor Development Program in India.

Stefan Rau of Jilin Yanji Low Carbon Climate Resilient Healthy City Project in the People's Republic of China.

Won Myong Hong and Santoshi Ishii of the Binh Duong Water Treatment Expansion Project in Viet Nam.

Yihong Wang, Anqian Huang, Zhijia Rao, and Jinqiang Chen of the Climate Resilient and Smart Urban Water Infrastructure Project in the PRC.

Ricardo Carlos Barba of the Inclusive, Resilient and Sustainable Housing for Urban Poor Sector Project in Tamil Nadu, India.

Shuji Hashizume, Daniel Wiedmer, Deborah Robertson, and James G. Baker of Indorama Ventures Regional Blue Loan Project in Southeast Asia.

David Urbaneja-Furelos of Green Bond Project in Georgia; Mark R. Bezuijen, Erdenesaikhan Nyamjav, and Ongonsar Purev of Sustainable Tourism Development Project Phase 1 and 2 in Mongolia.

The editorial team was comprised of Melissa Alipalo, researcher, writer, and editorial facilitator; Terry Erle Clayton, copy editor; Nonie Villanueva, layout and composition artist; Ma. Theresa Mercado, proofreader; and Cherry Lynn Zafaralla, page proof checkers. The team is grateful for the guidance and support of the Department of Communications.

Abbreviations

ADB	Asian Development Bank
BIWASE	Binh Duong Water Environment Joint Stock Company
BRT	Bus rapid transit
COVID-19	Coronavirus disease
DPR	Detailed project report
EAPF	Public Management, Financial Sector
EARD	East Asia Department
ECEC	East Coast Economic Corridor
GDP	Gross domestic product
GGU	Georgia Global Utilities JSC
GMS	Greater Mekong Subregion
GWP	Georgian Water & Power
HACAMP	Healthy and age-friendly city action and management plan
HAU	Housing Authority Unit
HIA	Health impact assessment
IFC	International Finance Corporation
IFI	International finance institution
IVL	Indorama Ventures Global Services Limited
JFPR	Japan Fund for Prosperous and Resilient Asia and the Pacific
JICA	Japan International Cooperation Agency
KPI	Key performance indicator
LEAP	Leading Asia's Private Infrastructure Fund
LIBOR	London Inter-Bank Offered Rate
KLNP	Khuvsgul Lake National Park
kV	Kilovolt
m³/day	Cubic meters per day
MFF	Multibranched financing facility
MLD	Million liters per day
MW	Megawatt
OBNP	Onon-Balj National Park
O&M	Operations and maintenance
PBL	Project-based loan

PET	Polyethylene terephthalate
PRC	People's Republic of China
PRCM	PRC Resident Mission
PSOD	Private Sector Operations Department
rPET	Recycled PET
SARC	South Asia Regional Cooperation and Operations Coordination Division
SAUW	South Asia Urban and Water Division
SDCC	Sustainable Development and Climate Change Department
SDP	Sector development program
SERD	Southeast Asia Department
SZWG	Shenzhen Water (Group) Co., Ltd.
TNUHDB	Tamil Nadu Urban Habitat Development Board
TOD	Transit-oriented development
UMRC	Uzbekistan Mortgage Refinance Company
VCIC	Visakhapatnam–Chennai Industrial Corridor
VCICDP	Visakhapatnam–Chennai Industrial Corridor Development Program

Introduction

This publication features innovative and successful urban projects and is designed as a collection that can be added to over time.

Objective

This report evolved from the wealth of innovative designs and groundbreaking approaches used in ADB's urban operations. The case studies are meant to introduce fresh ideas and projects to urban operations staff who may be contemplating similar challenges or needs in their respective DMCs and technical fields. The case studies are meant to act as a springboard for further knowledge sharing events whereby project staff can hear from those involved in the projects featured in these case studies. They may also offer background for more informed discussions.

Selection of Case Studies

The case study projects were chosen because of their innovative design features and because they were important firsts for a Developing Member Country (DMC), sector, or ADB operational practices. This initial collection of project briefs was selected in consultation with the Urban Sector Committee which is made up of the regional urban and water divisions and the Private Sector Operations Department.

Knowledge Gathering Approach

To add to the publicly available project information at www.adb.org, project staff involved in the design of the projects were interviewed to elaborate on the factors that inspired the innovations. They were asked about their experience advocating for their plans both with DMC clients and within ADB. Innovation implies risk as well as opportunity, which lends itself to exceptional concern and hesitation, but these project officers offer glimpses of the rewards that come with patience, dialogue, and determination.

Structure of Case Study Contents

Each of the case studies follows a similar structure. Each case study opens with a summary of the financing and implementation arrangements. A brief statement on the development need begins each case study as the basis and rationale for the project. Each begins with an explanation of the basis and rationale for the project and highlights the development challenges that spurred the need for innovative thinking. In some cases, the DMC client had proposed a traditional approach that a project team leader believed rrisked producing underwhelming results. In other cases, a project team leader believed ADB's value was not being leveraged in the initial proposal. Although every need and every challenge has a solution or set of solutions, project staff had to identify the most practical solutions compatible with ADB's project parameters and financing options and expectations for poverty reduction and gender development. Finding solutions required innovations and firsts.

Through continuous dialogue, upstream development and research and inspired big-thinking, project teams successfully advocated innovations and collaborated their way to projects that broke new ground and paved new inroads into sectors and financing options. What was eventually designed, the project basics, are summarized to give readers an idea of how the ideas took final shape. Because the case study projects are in their nascent stages of implementation, results were not always available to report though initial results and indications of promise and impact were already evident in many cases. In the absence of proof of concept through results, the concerns for sustainability and impact are given attention. And finally, any notes on replication round out the case study. For more information on the case study project, links and contact information have been provided.

The Initial Nine Case Studies

Nine case studies were developed for this publication.

"How Upstream Programmatic Interventions Drive Industrial and Urban Transformation," based on the Visakhapatname-Chennai Industrial Corridor Development Program, with project staff Manoj Sharma, Akira Matsunaga, Pushkar Srivastava, and Ashwin Hosur Viswanath. ADB has been helping the Government of India develop its concept of economic corridors. Unlike the traditional transport corridor project, the industrial corridor is an infrastructure strategy for industrial, urban, and transportation development in and between high-potential cities along the corridor.

"How People-Friendly Urban Mobility and Green Sponge Infrastructure is Transforming a City," based on the Jilin Yanji Low-Carbon Climate Resilient Healthy City Project, with project staff Stefan Rau. This project combines transport-oriented development, sponge city approaches, and open space development to profoundly transform Yanji, an older city that has struggled with congestion, floods, and major wastage of resources. It is the first rapid bus transit project in the country's northeast. Improved sidewalks and added bicycle lanes will connect important centers along the bus rapid transit (BRT) route, industrial park developments and job centers in the east and west of the urban area, and link many residential districts with the city center, where there are business and retail centers, a high-speed rail station, government centers, Yanbian University, schools, hospitals, and parks.

"A First in Viet Nam's Water Sector: Utility Transitions to Nonsovereign Lending," based on the Binh Duong Water Treatment Expansion Project," with project staff Won Myong Hong and Satoshi Ishii. Binh Duong Water Environment Joint Stock Company (BIWASE) is one of the biggest water utilities in Viet Nam, 80% owned by non-government shareholders and listed on the stock exchange. It had benefited from ADB's sovereign (public) loan supports approved in 2001 and 2012. ADB's sovereign and nonsovereign lending teams worked together to transition the utility to a nonsovereign loan, a first for the country's water sector and ADB operations in Viet Nam.

"**Nonsovereign People's Republic of China (PRC) Loan Demonstrates Broad Integration of Smart Water Technologies,**" based on the Climate Resilient and Smart Urban Water Infrastructure Project in the PRC, with project staff Yihong Wang, Anqian Huang, Zhijia Rau, and Jinqiang Chen. ADB's East Asia Regional Department and the Private Sector Operations Department (PSOD) worked together with the Shenzhen Water (Group) Co., Ltd. to develop a project demonstrating private sector participation in sponge city and smart technology applications.

"**Beyond Slum Upgrades: How Affordable Housing Projects Build Resilient, Thriving Households,**" a project based on the Inclusive, Resilient, Sustainable Housing for Urban Poor Sector Project in Tamil Nadu, India, with project staff Ricardo Carlos Barba. Rarely is household relocation the primary development objective of an ADB-supported project, but in the case of this Tamil Nadu project, the government is developing its capacity to consult with low-income families living on harzardous land to safely relocate them to sites designed and developed to fit their needs. Private operations and maintenance contracts to protect housing assets and a small group coaching program for households are some of the strategies at work in the project design. Connecting housing development to regional corridor development, and equity investments to promote public-private partnerships are other project innovations.

"**ADB's First Blue Loan Intercepts Plastics from Landfills, Oceans through Recycling, and Reuse of Ubiquitous PET,**" a project based on the Indorama Ventures Regional Blue Loan Project, with project staff Shuji Hashizume, Daniel Wiedmer, Deborah Robertson, and James G. Baker. ADB's private sector and sovereign operations staff collaborated to enter the plastics market in a substantial way with ADB's first nonsovereign internationally verified blue loan. The project will expand plastic recycling operations of one of the world's largest recyclers and reuse producers of plastic beverage bottles.

"**Private Sector Team in Georgia Expands Green Bond Market in Asia, Urban Water Sector,**" based on the Georgia Green Bond Project, with project staff David Urbaneja-Furelos. Outside developing countries, green bonds have proven to be a popular, innovative financial instrument for investments in environmental or climate-benefitting projects. They are noted for offering investors transparency and accountability. A team from ADB's PSOD proved green bonds to be an answer to one Georgian water utility's issue with tightening liquidity of the capital markets as a result of the Coronavirus disease (COVID-19) pandemic.

"**Integrating Urban Design, Nature, and Heritage for Tourism in a Cold-Climate Country: Preliminary ADB Lessons from Mongolia,**" based on the Mongolia Sustainable Tourism Project, with project staff Mark R. Bezuijen, Ongonsar Purev, and Erdenesaikhan Nyamjav. Tourism development is an emerging investment area of ADB in general and specifically eco-tourism in Mongolia, where ADB and the government are working together to bolster the industry through integrated tourism development. The projects aim to bring ecological and economic needs surrounding eco-tourism into alignment and direct tourism benefits toward poor and vulnerable residents. The project is also employing the Excellence in Design for Greater Efficiencies (EDGE)—an international green building design standard—to improve energy efficiency in the feasibility designs, construction and operation of a rock art research and tourist center.

"**The Making of a Market-Based Mortgage Sector,**" based on Uzbekistan's Mortgage Market Sector Development Program, with project staff Peter Barro and Bobir Baisovich Gafurov. To create a commercial mortgage market and reform current public housing programs, the ADB project team proposed a mix of financing and technical assistance to establish a wholesale mortgage refinance company that would offer banks long-term, fixed-rate local currency funds to enable more residential mortgage loan products, among other sector development activities.

Factors Motivating Innovation

Needing to add more value. Many of the team leaders interviewed for the selected case studies attributed their own innovative thinking to opportunities they identified for adding more ADB value to a DMC client's initial proposal. In these cases, the government requests for financing often involved traditional approaches, although experience with those approaches had either proved less sustainable than expected, were incommensurate with current sector challenges or did not harness opportunities with new technology, financing products, or good practices. The team leaders demonstrated a drive to be more than just a loan broker. They were determined to apply ADB's financial and knowledge resources to resolving a market or sector issue.

- See page 17, "How People-Friendly Urban Mobility and Green Sponge Infrastructure is Transforming a City," led by Stefan Rau
- See page 49, "Beyond Slum Upgrades: How Affordable Housing Projects Build Resilient, Thriving Households led by Ricardo Carlos Barba
- See page 89, "The Making of a Market-Based Mortgage Sector," led by Peter Marro and Bobir Baisovich Gafurov

The right key performance indicator incentivizes innovations. As part of its corporate strategy, ADB shifted one of its key performance indicators (KPI) away from the value of a loan to emphasize the volume of loans processed by its Private Sector Operations Department (PSOD). Prior to the KPI change, PSOD's mode of prioritizing clients had been about allocating limited staff resources as efficiently as possible. But with the internal emphasis on numbers of loans rather than the value of loans, PSOD has an incentive to broaden its scope of interest, which has meant working with smaller private entities and in new sectors. To achieve the KPI, PSOD has worked more closely with ADB's regional sovereign lending operational departments, who understand the sectoral issues and have access to potential clients, such as newly privatized utilities that need both financial and technical assistance. Working with smaller clients in sectors new to PSOD has demonstrated ADB's value in new market subsectors and helped build investor confidence.

- See page 31, "A First in Viet Nam's Water Sector: Utility Transitions to Nonsovereign Lending," with Won Myong Hong and Satoshi Ishii.

Demonstration value. Whether the innovation at work was for a new ADB-client relationship, a sector breakthrough, new strategy, or financial product, the prospect of demonstrating the successful innovation was a major, mutual motivation for both ADB and, typically, private sector clients. The case studies include examples of private clients gaining market potential as a result of securing ADB's more stringent financing or being able to demonstrate its value to development as a result of ADB financing. ADB has also been able to demonstrate its partnership potential in sectors and DMCs where PSOD had not been operating.

- See page 41, "Nonsovereign PRC Loan Demonstrates Broad Integration of Smart Water Technologies," with Yihong Wang, Anqian Huang, Zhijia Rao, and Jinqiang Chen.

One ADB teams. Several of the case studies are projects processed by One ADB teams, bringing together staff from sovereign and nonsovereign operations as well as from multiple sectors and themes. The One ADB teams offer DMC governments an opportunity to benefit from the collective efforts and resources from across ADB. Prior to the change in PSOD's KPI, project officers said staff from sovereign and nonsovereign operations did not have much opportunity to work together. When the KPI changed, sovereign lending staff could introduce potential clients to PSOD. Sovereign operational staff brought sector, DMC, and client knowledge to the project team while PSOD brought new financing products.

> ↪ See page 7, "How Upstream, Programmatic Interventions Drive Industrial and Urban Transformation" with Manoj Sharma, Akira Matsunaga, Pushkar Srivastava, and Ashwin Hosur Viswanath.

Lessons from Experience with Innovations

Project officers offered advice on developing innovative ideas with internal and DMC clients (government or private sector) with innovative ideas. Because innovations often involve a new approach, risk is inherent and can require more dialogue and time for project preparation. Here are a few of the more general recommendations staff had to offer.

Consult with world-class experts for designing projects in emerging areas, new markets. Project officers should consider the stakes involved in solving major macro-level social and economic problems when the solutions have a large-scale impact. The most difficult problems will attract the best minds. Do not hesitate to involve global experts in the project concept and design phases.

The best ideas may have to wait for the right people and time to get a "yes." Some of the case study projects experienced political change during the project preparation. Be ready to expect challenges from political change. Ideas and plans will need to be explained again to develop renewed political support and ownership of a project when there is a change in leadership in the government.

Secure more effective government engagement through close collaboration and communication. A close client relationship comes from listening to how clients understand their development challenges. Discuss ideas for project design that delivers optimal benefits in the time and with the funds available

Urban planners are an asset. In addition to ADB sector specialists, consider adding to project teams staff with planning backgrounds or generalists who can function as integration specialists. Conversely, DMCs and cities where planning systems are weaker should have mission leaders who can envision opportunities and can engage in effective consultations with government on integrating investments for greater synergies and co-benefits.

Improve project design and appraisal methodologies. Proposing more complex ideas, such as nature-based solutions, may be a very real challenge to DMC governments, engineers and contractors who may still favor gray over green infrastructure. The challenge of gaining consensus and preventing inertia during project preparation can be overcome through evidence from successful projects and methods that quantify economic benefits.

Co-financing can make the investment graduation more affordable for smaller clients. New, smaller private sector clients may feel more comfortable with ADB's nonsovereign lending terms if co-financing is introduced to minimize the loan yet still allow them to use ADB's due diligence, safeguards, and technical assistance.

Nonrefundable grants help clients move to nonsovereign projects. A nonrefundable technical assistance grant attached to a nonsovereign loan is unusual but may be effective in transitioning newly privatized municipal services from sovereign loan support to more commercial finance. The technical assistance grant for certain nonsovereign projects is also a vehicle for ADB's PSOD to deliver value-added, development benefits.

INDIA

Visakhapatnam–Chennai Industrial Corridor Development Program

1

How Upstream Programmatic Interventions Drive Industrial and Urban Transformation

with Manoj Sharma, Akira Matsunaga, Pushkar Srivastava, and Ashwin Hosur Viswanath

Project Name	Visakhapatnam–Chennai Industrial Corridor Development Program
Project Location	Regionally across the state of Andhra Pradesh, India
ADB Team	South Asia Urban and Water Division (SAUW)
Sector	Industry and trade, energy, water and other urban infrastructure and services (Subsectors: Large and medium industries, electricity transmission and distribution, non-urban road transport and urban water supply)
Year Approved	2016
Borrower	Government of India
Loan Amount	$625 million
Grant Amount	$5 million (Urban Climate Change Resilience Trust Fund under the Urban Financing Partnership Facility Grant)
Financing Modalities	Multi-tranche Financing Facility, OCR: $500 million
Project Scope	Support the state government's industrial development with financing and technical support that will establish a management corporation to oversee business-friendly processes for investors and manufacturers, while also financing basic infrastructure needs within industrial and residential areas and ensuring policies, reforms, institutional development, and workforce training are in place.
Risk Categorization	Complex
Design Team Leader(s)	Manoj Sharma, presently Chief of the Urban Sector Group
Current Project Officer	Akira Matsunaga, Senior Urban Development Specialist
Executing Agency	Department of Industries, Government of Andhra Pradesh

The Development Need

Every year, 12 million young people in India enter the labor force, yet rapid economic growth has not produced enough jobs.

Development Challenges

- Economic strategies have prioritized the service sector over manufacturing.
- The country's manufacturing potential is undermined by a lack of skilled labor, an 'unfriendly' policy and regulatory environment, and insufficient infrastructure.

Successful economic reforms in India in the 1990s produced rapid economic growth, but growth has proven insufficient for the country's dramatic demographic tilt toward a young working population needing jobs the economy has not provided.

"India tried to jump the gun and go from an agrarian economy to a services-led economy and realized that is not the right policy," said Manoj Sharma, Chief of the Urban Sector Group at the Asian Development Bank (ADB). "A country the size of India cannot skip industrial development. Maybe smaller countries could do that, but not India."

Project-based Solutions

Manufacturing is a proven creator of jobs and growth and would suit India's population dynamics. Understanding industry's potential to better address the scale of the country's population and employment prompted the current government to launch in 2014 the 'Make in India' policy to promote large-scale manufacturing. Connectivity to regional trade markets is key to attracting investors and growth. In 2013, India's share of world trade reached only 2% because of low engagement with global production networks. Neighboring countries are using these networks to manufacture and sell components rather than finished products, thereby surpassing India's manufacturing growth and output levels.

Innovations and Firsts

Since 2012, ADB has been helping the Government of India develop its concept of economic corridors to connect the country's five largest cities.

Unlike the traditional transport corridor project, the industrial corridor is an infrastructure strategy for industrial, urban, and transportation development in and between high-potential cities within the corridor (Figure 1). The approach refers to these cities as nodes, a linguistic signifier of their role in a larger economic context. They are not just independent cities but an important link and a strategically developed element of an extended urban belt within the corridor. Each city, or node, serves as a logistics hub. Industrial parks, energy generation, and transport are critical facets of each node city for connecting trade links.

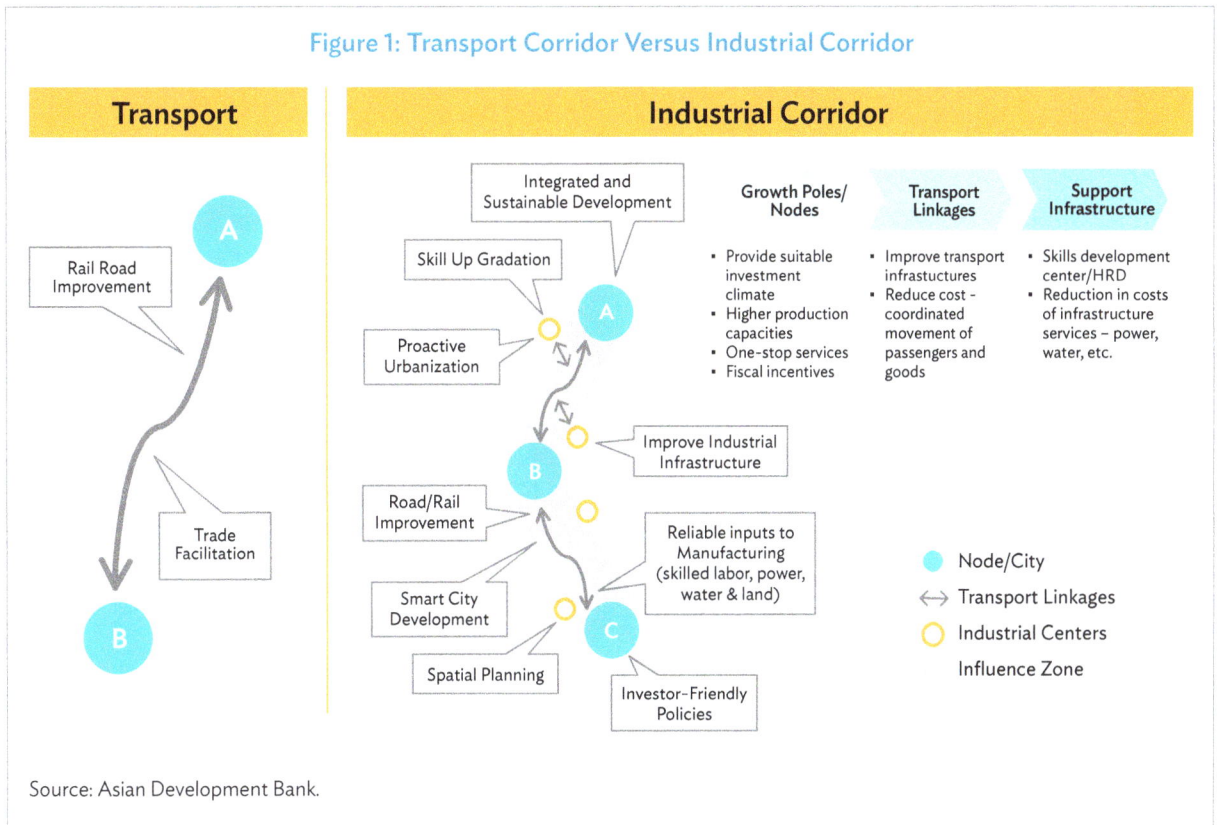

Figure 1: Transport Corridor Versus Industrial Corridor

Source: Asian Development Bank.

"This is proactive urbanization. Once you set up these nodes, you invite the private sector, and that's where the jobs come from, but the governance of these areas is very important," Sharma said. "There should be policy, infrastructure, jobs, and quality living conditions with spaces to live, work, and play. This is a livable city. For jobs to be possible, there needs to be a labor force, capital, and talent."

Of the five corridors identified, ADB is supporting the East Coast Economic Corridor (ECEC), which stretches 2,500 kilometers (km) from Kolkata, West Bengal in the north, to Tuticorin, Tamil Nadu in the south.

 This is proactive urbanization. Once you set up these nodes, you invite the private sector—that's where the jobs come from, but the governance of these areas is very important.

— Manoj Sharma, chief, Urban Sector Group

ADB is supporting the middle stretch of the ECEC called the Visakhapatnam-Chennai Economic Corridor (VCIC), an 800-km stretch of coastline that connects four economic hubs and nine industrial clusters. This makes it a strategic trade location for industrial production and creates seamless trade links with regional production chains and global production networks in Southeast and South Asia. The VCIC is in Andhra Pradesh, one of India's most prosperous states, largely because of its pharmaceutical exports. Over 50% of the world's pharmaceuticals are produced in India. The VCIC is one of the country's most promising opportunity for port-led economic growth.

The VCIC consist of eleven nodes (Figure 2). Ideally, most nodes are developed from greenfield spaces (uninhabited, agriculturally unproductive large land tracts). The nodes are developed to host specific manufacturing specialties. For example, the Visakhapatnam node is the anchor node and focuses on pharmaceuticals, textiles, chemicals, petrochemicals and steel manufacturing, while the Kakinada node focuses on ICT hardware and has plans for food processing and paper production. The Gannavaram node is dedicated to agricultural and food processing and textiles, while the southernmost node of Srikalahasti-Yerpedu, which is less conceptualized than other nodes, could focus on electrical equipment and capitalize on its coastal location and proximity to the Chennai airport for strategic tourism development.

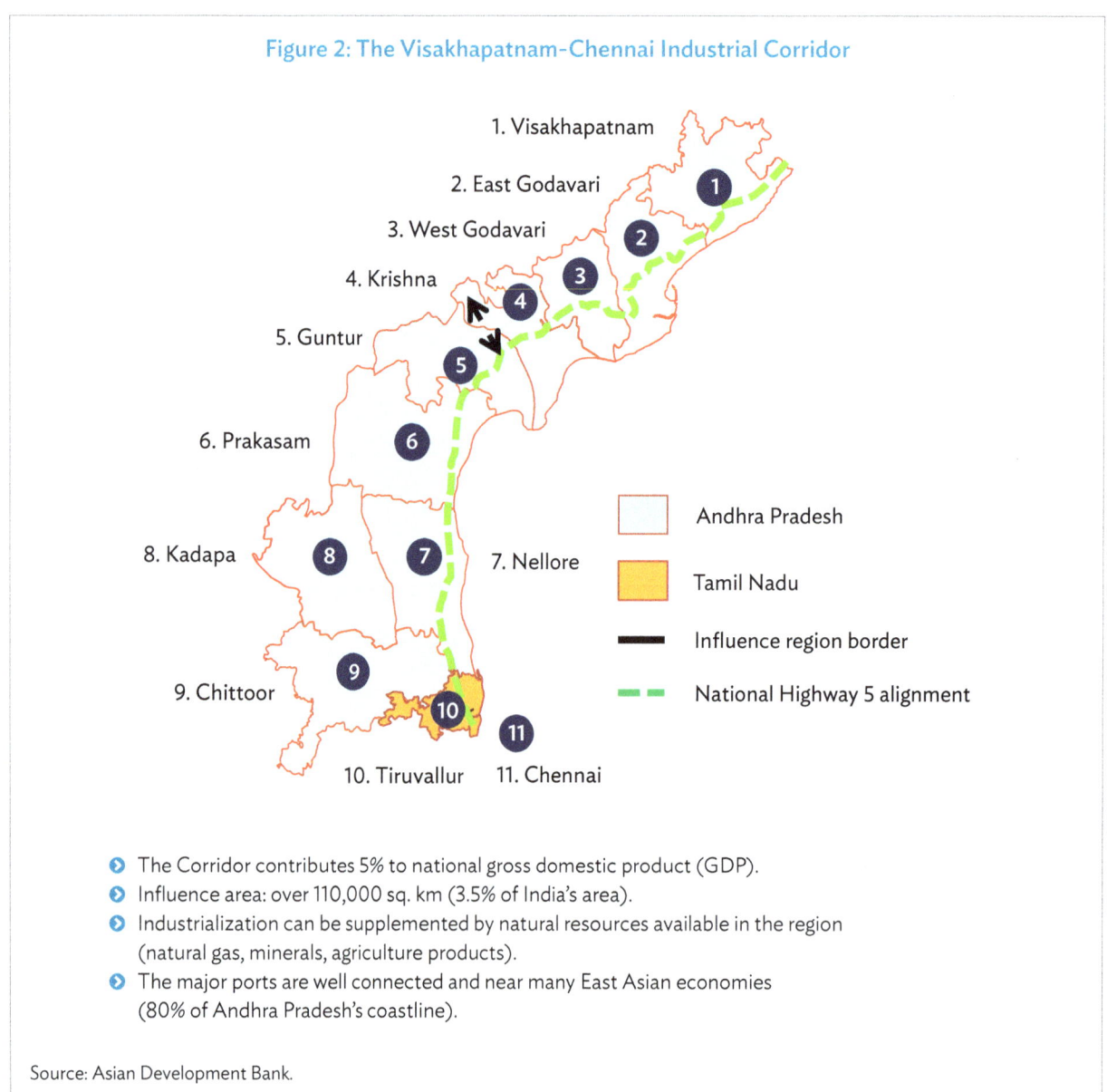

Figure 2: The Visakhapatnam-Chennai Industrial Corridor

- The Corridor contributes 5% to national gross domestic product (GDP).
- Influence area: over 110,000 sq. km (3.5% of India's area).
- Industrialization can be supplemented by natural resources available in the region (natural gas, minerals, agriculture products).
- The major ports are well connected and near many East Asian economies (80% of Andhra Pradesh's coastline).

Source: Asian Development Bank.

Advocating for Innovation

The industrial corridor approach was a new concept for ADB. The idea for the VCIC project came from ADB's South Asia Regional Cooperation and Operations Coordination Division (SARC), not the project operations staff. In 2013, SARC began analyzing the ECEC and the existing policy environment to understand the development mechanics and potential to generate quality growth, jobs, incomes, and sustained development.

The following year, SARC, which was then headed by Sekhar Bonu, conducted a feasibility study of the ECEC that identified three phases, one of which was the VCIC. SARC then prepared a conceptual development plan for the VCIC. The study identified four nodes for Phase 1 based on five criteria: (i) current level of industrial agglomeration, (ii) availability of land for development of new industrial clusters, (iii) proximity to urban centers and seaports, (iv) rail and road connectivity, and (v) availability of power and water. "This is when the project began to take real shape," said Pushkar Srivastava, ADB's project management specialist.

The multi-sector nature of the project required collaboration across the ADB. Team members were drawn from South Asia Urban and Water Division (SAUW), energy, and SARC, demonstrating the One ADB concept. For example, the first tranche of the multibranched financing facility (MFF) involved connecting an important port to a state highway by extending it by 30 kilometers. Since the project was launched, investments in smart water management systems in Visakhapatnam have reduced nonrevenue water and provided continuous supply. Seven power substations have been upgraded and an effluent treatment facility constructed.

The project design is based on the theory that infrastructure coupled with reforms will produce jobs and growth, both of which are needed to address India's demographic challenges.

Along the VCIC, ADB supports each node city in various ways including, (i) the development of an infrastructure strategy, (ii) identification of key industries and sectors, (iii) creating investment plans, and (iv) implementing policy reforms that will attract investors and industry. In the early conceptual phase of the project, drone surveys were undertaken for mapping and to identify infrastructure needs. "We also looked at where people would settle to know the infrastructure needs there," Srivastava said.

The policy-based loan offers the government financial incentives for implementing agreed reforms based on best practices to ease doing business, develop investor programs, enhance local labor market skills, and offer institutional development to support the corridor. Business-friendly reforms include streamlined approval for business ventures and a single-window method for processing clearances. The sole authority for the node is the Andhra Pradesh Industrial Corridor Development Act.

Project Details

In September 2016, ADB approved $631 million in support for the VCIC, including an MFF, a policy-based loan, a technical assistance grant, and a grant from the Urban Climate Change and Resilience Trust Fund as the VCIC coastline is highly vulnerable to cyclones. The project aims to create industry-friendly policies and processes and reliable infrastructure and connectivity within and across the corridor to support industrial logistics and a skilled workforce.

"The project was ahead of its time. It wasn't just multi-sector development. The project integrated the sectors for regional development, not just urban development," Sharma said. The project integrated transport, power, other city infrastructure, and skills development. The issue then was, which ADB division within SARD should be responsible? The project would be implemented with a variety of government agencies and departments and there was no single focal department.

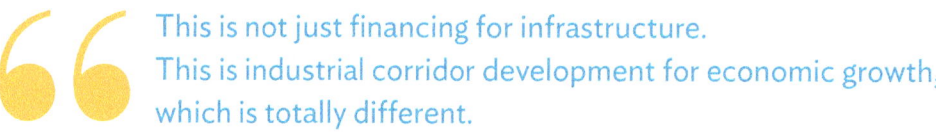

> This is not just financing for infrastructure. This is industrial corridor development for economic growth, which is totally different.
>
> — Akira Matsunaga, senior urban development specialist

For the first time in ADB operations and with special management approval, the project designers also combined an MFF for infrastructure with a project-based loan (PBL) for reforms.

"This is not just financing for infrastructure. This is industrial corridor development for economic growth, which is totally different," said Akira Matsunaga, Senior Urban Development Specialist for SAUW. "With typical municipal infrastructure, like water supply and power, the demand is normally there. The users are already there. With industrial development, there is policy competition." The state needs to attract investors by creating an enabling environment for investment. It should include not only infrastructure development but also investor outreach programs, marketing, and a single-desk policy for business processing and skills development.

The project is organized to produce three outputs. Output 1 aims to strengthen corridor management by establishing and supporting management to provide a business-friendly environment and processes for manufacturers. Output 2 improves the infrastructure, both internally within node cities and externally between nodes. Output 3 supports the project implementation and effectiveness through institutional capacity building and workforce skills development that would match the nodal industrial employment market. The MFF and Urban Climate Change Resilience Trust Fund. grant support priority infrastructure investments in the VCIC, and the PBL and technical assistance support policy reforms and institutional development in the state.

Policy development and reform. The PBL is disbursed in two tranches, each totaling $62.5 million. The release of each tranche is contingent on the satisfactory implementation of 12 policy reforms per tranche related to corridor management and ease of doing business.

Climate change resilience. The Urban Climate Change Resilience Trust Fund provided $5 million to pilot new technologies in Visakhapatnam because Andhra Pradesh is vulnerable to cyclones. The project will install a 3 megawatt (MW) floating solar facility on a lake that will provide renewable energy with zero land footprint and reduces lakewater evaporation. Other nature-based solutions are being tested to rehabilitate the lake to augment drinking water storage capacity. Piloting e-vehicles will provide clean and low carbon municipal solid waste management services.

In 2018, SARC further finalized the Visakhapatnam-Chennai Industrial Corridor Development Program (VCICDP) master plan, which prioritized one northern and one southern node, conducted industry assessments, and identified priority projects. The target industries were shortlisted in each node using specific criteria (global production network links to the existing manufacturing sector, high industrial sector growth projections, and competitiveness of industry location). The ADB design team studied industrial parks and manufacturing developments in Republic of Korea, Japan, and the People's Republic of China. The MFF is divided into two financing tranches. The scope of the second tranche is being discussed with the state government along with this master plan. "ADB could not have done more to help manufacturing development in Andhra Pradesh," Matsunaga said.

The long-term engagement supported by various ADB instruments can draw a high level of commitment from the government and enable their continuous improvement through active dialogue and interventions. The programmatic approach of VCICDP highlighted the value of (i) having a long-term platform and strategic focus to guide policy dialogues, (ii) high-level government commitment to push for reforms, and (iii) active interactions to maximize the consolidated development impacts. Interventions can evolve over time during the program period, reflecting lessons learned from the prior phase (BOX 1). Policy dialogues identify the required actions to implement reforms and the joint technical and institutional review entails corrective actions to ensure service delivery. The success of prior interventions can be scaled and institutionalized to bring broader changes in subsequent phases.

BOX 1

Summary of Intended Results for the India Visakhapatnam–Chennai Industrial Corridor Development Program

OUTCOME

Enhanced growth and competitiveness of the Visakhapatnam–Chennai Industrial Corridor (VCIC). By 2025:
- Manufacturing sector output in Andhra Pradesh increased to INR 4.2 trillion ($64 billion). 2015 baseline: INR 1 trillion ($16 billion).
- Gross value added per person in the manufacturing sector increased to INR 1.0 million. 2013 baseline: INR 0.483 million per person engaged.[a]
- Average daily employment of women in factories in Andhra Pradesh increased to 18%. 2010 baseline for Andhra Pradesh: 13%[b]
- 24-hour power supply available for all manufacturing firms in the VCIC and interruption duration not to exceed 1 hour a month for feeders in at least 2 VCIC industrial clusters. 2016 baseline: 24-hour power supply not available for all manufacturing firms in the VCIC and interruption duration exceeded 5 hours a month.
- 24-hour drinking water supply provided to 64,800 households and nonrevenue water reduced to less than 15% in the project area in Visakhapatnam. 2015 baseline: 0 for 24-hour supply not available and nonrevenue water at 50%.
- Traffic in VCIC increased to 21,000 passenger car units. 2015: baseline: 15,000 passenger car units.

OUTPUT 1

Stronger corridor management and improved ease of doing business. By 2024:
- Corridor management institutions established and operational.
- State's rating remains in top five on ease of doing business.
- New e-portal and single-desk system issues business-related licenses to over 90% of the applicants.
- New industrial and sector policies notified and implemented with fiscal incentives and special packages for women entrepreneurs.

OUTPUT 2

Stronger, more resilient infrastructure for VCIC. By 2024:
- 45 km of internal roads improved, with gender-responsive design features[c] and 47 km of storm water drains constructed in industrial clusters.
- Four million liters per day (MLD) common effluent treatment plants constructed in industrial clusters.
- 123 km of pipelines, 27 MLD water treatment plants, and 9,100 million liters of storage tanks constructed in industrial clusters.
- 94 km of state highways widened, with gender-responsive design features.
- New substations (one 400 by 220 kilovolt followed (kV), five 220 by 132 kV, and four 132 by 33 kV) with a capacity of about 3,170 MVA and related transmission network comprising about 240 km of overhead and 41 km of underground transmission and distribution lines of 400, 220, and 132 kV installed for industrial clusters.
- 365 km of new drinking water pipelines constructed or rehabilitated, and 64,800 water meters installed in Visakhapatnam.
- Climate change resilience plan for Visakhapatnam prepared and adopted for integrated water management solutions.

OUTPUT 3

Stronger institutional capacities, human resources, and program. By 2025:
- Project development mechanism with time-bound action plan established.
- At least 25,000 persons (at least 20% women) have completed skills training for VCIC jobs.
- 500 staff of executing and implementing agencies (including all women staff) have attended capacity development programs, including training on gender and monitoring of gender-disaggregated data.
- Investor promotion plan developed and implemented on time.
- Satisfactory quarterly program reviews and audit reports submitted on time (gender-disaggregated data collected).

---

[a] Government of India, Ministry of Statistics and Programme Implementation. 2015. *Annual Survey of Industries, 2012–2013*. Kolkata (Statement 9B, Sections 5-8).

[b] Government of India, Ministry of Labour and Employment. 2014. Statistical Profile on Women Labour, 2012–2013. Chandigarh/Shimla (Table 2.2, page 28).

[c] Gender-responsive design features for roads include walking paths, separate toilets for women, telephone helplines, adequate lighting, signage, demarcated road crossings, and safe public spaces.

Notes: kV = kilovolt, MVA = mega volt ampere.
Source: ADB. 2016. *Proposed Multibranched Financing Facility, Policy-Based Loan, Technical Assistance Grant, and Administration of Grant, Report and Recommendations to the President: India: Visakhapatnam-Chennai Industrial Corridor Development Program*. Manila.

Concerns for Sustainability and Impact

By 2025, investments should have increased annual industrial output by 400%, from $16 billion annually in 2015 to $64 billion in 2025. The MFF is scheduled to be completed by the end of 2025, with the first project completed by December 2023. Both tranches of the PBL ($62.5 million each) have been disbursed for 12 policy action items for each tranche.

If the planned investments and reforms take place and are followed by persistent and consolidated efforts of the state government, by 2045, Andhra Pradesh will have increased its gross domestic product (GDP) by six times, its manufacturing output by seven times, and job growth by five times. For this to happen, the government must successfully appeal to and secure investors in manufacturing. Various ADB departments and divisions are collaborating on strategic domestic and foreign investor outreach to promote the government's efforts with the VCIC.

Andhra Pradesh was already a successful investor destination, so the challenge has not been as difficult as it could be for other corridors. Andhra Pradesh ranks first for ease of doing business in India. India has moved up in the World Bank's international ranking for ease of doing business, from 130 to 100 in 2017. Andhra Pradesh's economy grew an average of 7% from 2005 to 2015 but industrial output was low, only 12% of the state's GDP, lagging the national manufacturing average of 15%.

India's National Manufacturing Policy (2012) aims to increase manufacturing from 15% to 25% and create 100 million jobs by 2022. The policy depends on the government's economic corridor approach to attracting manufacturing investments and creating jobs resulting from improved infrastructure within and between manufacturing nodes. This will assure manufacturers of efficient transportation, reliable utility services (roads, water, power, drainage, effluent treatment, etc.), and business-friendly policies and processes.

The VCIC is the most advanced of the corridor projects in terms of economic potential, development readiness, and integrated development design. There are synergies between the PBL and MFF while the node cities and surrounding urban clusters are growing as an urban-industrial ecosystem.

The state of Andhra Pradesh has made substantial progress in implementing transformative reforms to improve corridor management and ease of doing business. The institutional foundation has been put in place, with the state agency assuming sole responsibility for regulating corridor development and special purpose vehicles implementing industrial estate plans. The state has initiated investor promotion through vigorous marketing activities and providing an enabling environment for industry by providing incentives to investors, establishing a statewide single-desk, and training for skills development. The ongoing infrastructure improvement works include development of connector roads, power supply, bulk water supply, internal infrastructure within the clusters, and climate resilient infrastructure. This quality infrastructure will attract the industries associated with various policies and actions for investment promotion under the PBL.

Success and sustainability of the economic corridor requires investor acquisition. ADB is helping the state government promote Andhra Pradesh regionally to attract investors. Equally important is the state government's continued commitment to its priority objective. ADB continues its dialogue with the state government to help maximize the development impact and realize the state's vision of becoming a globally competitive destination for investment.

Notes on Replication

ADB has replicated variations of the industrial corridor approach elsewhere in India, Sri Lanka, and Bangladesh. In India, the Chennai-Kanyakumari corridor is part of the East Coast Economic Corridor (ECEC), where ADB is implementing sector projects. ADB is also designing a corridor program in India's landlocked northeast region and connecting it through development of identified rail and road connectivity projects coupled with facility augmentation of land ports and the Chattogram port in Bangladesh. Other states have also requested ADB's support for industrial development projects. ADB staff interviewed for this case study offered these recommendations:

- Upstream study is key to identifying and planning large-scale, integrated development projects.
- Programmatic interventions with active policy dialogues can evolve over time during the program period, reflecting lessons learned from the prior phase and identifying the required actions.
- Advance project preparations by the EA/IA advance the work considerably, especially the detailed project reports. The time to prepare the project was halved because the state government took the initiative and bore the costs of the DPRs. "Mission leaders should encourage the implementing agencies to prepare the DPRs in advance," Srivastava said.
- In addition to sector specialists, ADB would benefit from integration specialists.
- Any new water system should use smart water technology and smart management. Mid-project, the Greater Visakhapatnam Municipal Corporation opted to upgrade the project technology for the water supply system to smart water meters that allow for real-time remote meter reading for continuous monitoring, real-time leak detection, and rapid response for leak repairs. The Municipal Corporation absorbed the cost difference, but Srivastava believes that a fuller cost benefit analysis of smart water management systems would have proven more cost effective due to averted losses in nonrevenue water losses. "This should be taken up in any new water infrastructure project," Srivastava advised.
- Project schedules benefit from simple procurement measures, as did this project. For example, the first MFF tranche was limited to six civil works packages for international competitive bidding. The implementing agency demonstrated a high level of readiness from the beginning, having completed all of its DPRs before ADB's project approval.

Learn More

Read more detailed background on the project development in Scaling New Heights: Vizag-Chennai Industrial Corridor India's First Coastal Corridor.

Contact: Akira Matsunaga,
Senior Urban Development Specialist
amatsunaga@adb.org

THE PEOPLE'S REPUBLIC OF CHINA

The Jilin Yanji Low Carbon Climate Resilient Healthy City Project

How People-Friendly Urban Mobility and Green Sponge Infrastructure is Transforming a City

with Stefan Rau

Project Name	The Jilin Yanji Low-Carbon Climate Resilient Healthy City Project
Project Location	Yanji City, Jilin Province, The People's Republic of China
ADB Team	Urban and Social Sectors Division, East Asia Regional Department
Sector	Urban Transport, Flood Protection, Water Supply, Sanitation
Year Approved	December 2019
Borrower	Government of the People's Republic of China
Loan Amount	$130 million equivalent
Financial Modalities	Ordinary Capital Resources
Project Scope	Improve public transport and urban functions by reducing congestion, improving pedestrian and bicycle networks, reducing flooding in the city, and improving water safety and security and positive health outcomes. The project applies nature-based solutions integrating green spaces with hydraulic functions and ecological restoration.
Risk Categorization	Low Risk
Design Team Leader(s)	Stefan Rau, Senior Urban Development Specialist (also the current project officer)
Executing Agency	Yanji City Government

The Development Need

Yanji City in Jilin Province needed to become livable again. But where to begin? What development strategy and investment by ADB could make a significant, long-term difference to the health, vibrancy, and productivity of the city and its residents? Traffic congestion and perennial urban flooding had become major debilitating factors.

Development Challenges

Yanji had been experiencing a general economic slowdown, like many medium-size cities in the PRC's northeast. No single problem was at the root of the challenges residents faced in trying to improve their lives or by companies trying to invest in the city. There were the obvious problems of traffic and urban flooding, and the less obvious but still very real problems of the city's aging underground water and drainage infrastructure and missing transportation links. No single solution could transform the daily life and struggles of pedestrians, commuters, and residents.

Traffic. Individuals with financial means overcame their problems with the city's inefficient public transportation system by purchasing private vehicles. Vehicle registration in Yanji increased 57% between 2012 and 2017. The increase in cars contributed to other problems: increasing traffic, air pollution, and even less walkable streets because of cars parked on sidewalks. Public transportation was mainly by buses, which had to contend with a small bus fleet, heavy traffic, and congested routes. Bus routes were limited to six main streets and did not extend sufficiently into the periphery. Passengers had to accept other realities of public transportation in Yanji. One was often left waiting in the cold or the rain due to a lack of bus shelters and bus terminals and unreliable schedules. There were few bicycle lanes and the network of pedestrian sidewalks and paths to the limited green spaces and greenways were fragmented.

Flooding. If the traffic situation was difficult, imagine what happened in the city and to commuters during the June-July rainy season when some roads and urban areas are regularly flooded. The city floods an annual average of five days, endangering health and lives, threatening property and livelihoods with loss, and disturbing productivity in the city until the water recedes and people can get back to business. The sewer and drainage pipe system were combined and outdated. Only 12% of the pipe network met the domestically required 1-in-3-year flood design standards, causing prolonged flooding during heavy summer rains. The current flood risk for the Chaoyang River catchment is only designed to withstand 1-in-20-year flood events.

Drinking water losses. Jilin Yanji's water supply meets national quality standards and is available around the clock, but at a cost to the city that is invisible to most customers. Beneath the city, aged pipes in unknown locations were leaking as much as 37% of the water supplied from the city's treatment plants. Another 9% of water went unpaid by users. The difficulty in repairing leaks was typical of aged pipes, most laid in the 1930s and 1970s. It was difficult to locate pipes because plans of the underground system, which needs to be far below the surface due to extreme winter temperatures, have been lost.

The impact on residents was not just inconvenience but also health and safety issues created by pollution, flood waters, poorly planned and managed streets and parking that pedestrians and cyclists had to contend with daily. Taken together, the city's traffic conditions and overall environment made the city an unnecessarily difficult place to live and work.

Project-based Solutions

To address Yanji's congestion, floods, and major waste of resources, the city needed a large-scale, multi-sector integrated urban investment plan that would consider the connection between the city's challenges and how to develop integrated solutions that create synergies and co-benefits. A systematic approach would aim at tangible improvements (Figure 3).

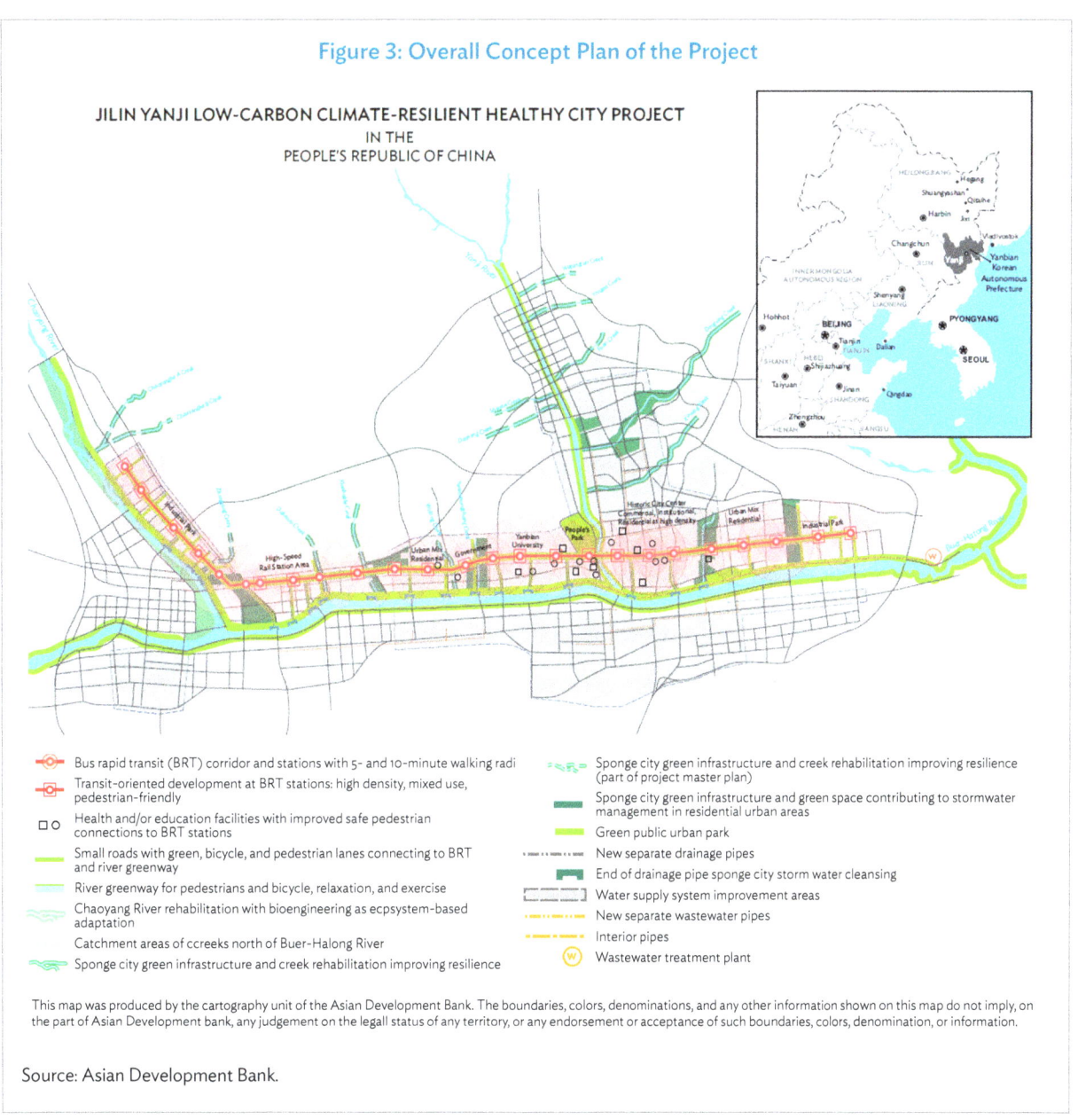

Figure 3: Overall Concept Plan of the Project

Source: Asian Development Bank.

Innovations and Firsts

- Integration of transit-oriented development and open spaces as sponge city green infrastructure.
- First bus rapid transit (BRT) corridor of its kind in northeast People's Republic of China (PRC).
- Advanced design and systemic integration of sponge city green and gray drainage pipe infrastructure.
- Positive health and age-inclusive outcomes from development of healthy and age-friendly action plan.

> In urban development we often worked against nature. Now we need to incorporate the regulation capacity and benefits of nature as its force increases with a changing climate.
>
> — Stefan Rau, senior urban development specialist for East Asia Regional Department, ADB

Transit-oriented development. Transport, development and green spaces are key functions of a city. Transport-oriented development (TOD) has the potential to profoundly transform a city, even in older cities where zoning updates are needed, like in Yanji. Public transportation lines (light-rail, bus, train, etc.) are serviced by terminals and stations that set a tone, tempo, and expectations for urban life and mobility (Figure 4). Urban functions around transport terminals should be intense and radiate into the city's streets and side streets. "TOD is an opportunity for vibrant high-density, mixed-use center areas around stations and they require pedestrian friendly, age- and gender-inclusive public spaces where people feel safe and enjoy meeting others," Rau said.

Figure 4: Illustration of Rapid Bus Transit Station

Source: Asian Development Bank Project Management Office, Yanji City.

Sponge city. The sponge city approach applies water-related nature-based solutions and resilient green infrastructure. It aims at sustainable and resilient rain- and stormwater management through wetlands, water retention parks, rain gardens, bioswales,[1] pervious pavement, and green roofs to reduce urban flooding and reduce stormwater peak flows through retention, natural infiltration, rainwater harvesting and reuse (see Figure 5 for examples of sponge city and green infrastructure). The concept can be applied to existing cities and to new urban developments. Existing urban areas can be transformed through adding green infrastructure that retains and absorbs natural rainwater flows that can then naturally infiltrate into the ground and recharge the groundwater. The retained water can also be stored for industrial use, street cleaning and parkland irrigation, thereby keeping cityscapes lush and inviting for recreational space and emissions mitigation. The PRC began testing the concept of the sponge city in 2015 with 16 pilot cities around the country. ADB already supported river rehabilitation projects in the PRC, cleaning up water and rehabilitating river ecologies to maximize flood control and biodiversity enhancement.

In this project, TOD is integrated with the sponge city, green infrastructure, and open space development concepts, and together they are expected to contribute to a low carbon climate resilient future for Yanji. The sponge city green infrastructure is systemically integrated with gray infrastructure, like the drainage pipe network, and together they can effectively prevent future urban flooding.

"In urban development, we often worked against nature by building in floodplains and channeling rivers, Now we need to incorporate the regulation capacity and benefits of nature as its force increases with a changing climate, as we can see from increased flooding," Stefan Rau said. "There are challenges of acceptance and inertia when we try to apply and mainstream nature-based solutions. In most people's minds, infrastructure is gray; it's made of concrete or steel, and local decision makers, engineers and contractors need a lot of convincing that green infrastructure works. The great thing about these functional green spaces is they also deliver many other benefits for a city and its citizens. So building green infrastructure in our cities will deliver more resilience and health and less pollution and carbon emissions."

In 2015, Rau was the project team leader for one of ADB's first collaborations with the PRC on implementing the sponge city concept. The project demonstrates the sponge city approach through river rehabilitation, and each of ADB's investments in the sponge city approach since has improved the development and application of the concept in each project, Rau said.

---

[1] Bioswales are channels designed to concentrate and convey stormwater runoff while removing debris and pollution

Figure 5: Illustrations of Sponge City Green Infrastructure Planning and Examples

Note: Sponge city green infrastructure opening up a covered canal as an open creek receiving rainwater from newly installed residential raingardens.
Drawings and photos by Nengshi Zheng.
Source: Asian Development Bank.

Healthy and Age-Friendly City Action and Management Plan. The project team included the application of a health impact assessment (HIA) of the proposed project plans, from which a method and guideline was created to develop a Healthy and Age-Friendly City Action and Management Plan (HACAMP).[2] This new method is being applied to bring out further healthy and age-inclusiveness results for citizens. For example, the design of a sponge city with improved green spaces and improved public transport service will promote healthy lifestyles, walking, and cycling, which will, in turn, improve air quality and reduce summer heat island effects. Improved pedestrian safety and safe paths to schools, health and care facilities for older people, and exercise equipment in public spaces will benefit the old and the young. Improved water safety and security will ensure basic clean water service supply to all.

Standard economic analysis of development projects often falls short of quantifying costs and benefits of public health or ecosystem services. But both stand to gain a lot with improved and cleaner urban transit and green infrastructure and spaces. An HIA and HACAMP can also help quantify the value of benefits of a transit-oriented, pedestrian friendly, age-friendly sponge city. Residents, especially older people, children, and women can enjoy more hospitable and safe public spaces where they may have once felt vulnerable to either traffic accidents or urban crime in neglected public spaces.

---

2   https://www.adb.org/publications/healthy-age-friendly-cities-prc.

Advocating for Innovations

The city government's original proposal asked ADB to finance a list of priority standard infrastructure improvements, including a few urban roads, water, drainage, and sewer pipes in various areas around the city. Rau said, as an urban planner, he was looking for ADB's investment to add more value and contribute to the overall development of the city. He analyzed the city's geography, challenges, and opportunities and asked to see all government master and sector development plans and engaged with various local administrative bureaus and started to offer some new ideas.

While there was a public transport plan inclusive of BRT lines, the city did not consider it ready for implementation and had no funding assigned. The city had also prepared a sponge city concept for urban water management and flood protection and even applied for the national program but was not accepted. Rau developed a project concept that included and integrated these elements, with further development and strengthening of the plans.

With Rau as project team leader, ADB assembled a One ADB team of specialists and engaged transport, municipal engineering, environmental, social and climate change experts to carry out a demand analysis and a study for a BRT corridor and for improving flood risk management, sponge city green spaces and ecological river rehabilitation, incorporating climate risk assessment and adaptation.

"Engaging the right people and encouraging them to collaborate and work outside their comfort zones, I asked them to discuss with the government changes to land use around stations, such as adding more small streets with green spaces for walking and cycling, that would link to the river. Could we prepare a sponge city master plan for the whole city?" The consultants found the BRT idea to be highly feasible and capable of linking major urban functions such as a high-speed rail station, the city center, a university with 30,000 students, government centers, dense urban residential communities, and employees of two major industrial parks to the east and west. The BRT and the green sponge city infrastructure supports the city's master plan beyond the government's original proposal.

The government's commitment to the integrated urban planning and design project proposal grew over time. Government leaders and concerned bureaus eventually realized what the proposed project's synergies and benefits could offer to the overall development of Yanji and fully supported the ideas. "Without a good client, urban planners and designers cannot develop a good project" Rau said. At one critical milestone, the government considered canceling key components that had been agreed. The design was saved through a conversation about integrated approaches with high level local officials and how the investment would deliver great additional benefits.

"One thing I learned from this project is that you have to make sure the client doesn't just understand the approach but understands the significance of its impact and the various additional benefits from the integration across sectors," Rau said. Once the client truly understands the value of the design, the risk of project components being second-guessed becomes less likely. Integrated development requires understanding each piece as an important part of the whole. This is a challenge everywhere, and in the PRC, departmentalization is a strong feature in administrations.

Project Vision

The project was envisioned to help transform the city into a livable and inclusive, low carbon, resilient, efficient and inviting place centered along waterways with a transformed east to west urban corridor parallel to the Buer Hatong River. This would be the first BRT in the city and the first in northeast PRC. Improved sidewalks and added bicycle lanes would connect important centers along the BRT route, industrial park developments and job centers in the east and west of the urban area, and link many residential districts with the city center where there are business and retail centers, a high-speed rail station, government centers, Yanbian University, schools, hospitals, and parks.

The BRT stations will be linked to green spaces and project-supported riverfront greenways that promote healthier lifestyles for residents and tourists of all ages. Additional small streets and green spaces are designed as sponge city green infrastructure to reduce the risk of urban flooding. Improvements to the drainage and sewer systems are integrated with green infrastructure and together will greatly reduce flood risk and improve efficiencies. The water supply system will also be improved to reduce water losses and generate more water safety and security, saving an annual 4.8 million cubic meters of freshwater resources per year.

Project Details

The project's four integrated outputs generate co-benefits and higher efficiencies than if they were constructed as stand-alone projects without consideration for how they connect to other key infrastructure and environmental aspects of the city. Box 2 summarizes the four outputs and their targets.

The project includes the construction of a 20-kilometer BRT corridor, the anchor of the urban transformation to come from the project. The corridor will be serviced by 25 stations equipped with special features for people with disabilities and women waiting at the stations. These will include features such as wheelchair access, alarm buttons, priority seating, and safe lighting. Each station will be surrounded by at least five green space plazas with landscaping and exercise equipment for all ages.

The project will also finance the procurement of 100 clean energy BRT buses with priority seating for people with special needs, such as older people, pregnant women, and differently-abled. A central bus terminal and at least one command center for providing information services to operators is also part of the project package.

Residents will experience a more livable city even before their arrival at a bus station or without ever even using the BRT. The project is supporting the construction of at least 30 kilometers of pedestrian links to BRT stations, including safe crossings and routes to schools and hospitals with safe lighting. Sidewalk parking will be prohibited in at least six problematic locations along the BRT corridor and 100 new spaces provided near BRT stations along with park-and-ride lots. Cyclists will have access to at least 30 kilometers of dedicated bicycle lanes along the BRT route and links to BRT stations with bike-parking facilities.

Green Infrastructure to Ward off Flooding

The project will separate the drainage system from the wastewater system and add to residential areas various types of green infrastructure commonly associated with sponge city approaches, such as strategically built green spaces to retain and reuse storm water. This will reduce the risk of flooding in the city during the two-month rainy season. The green spaces will also host outdoor recreational areas for residents of all ages.

The project will improve water quality by constructing sedimentation tanks and reed-bed sand filters at the end of drainage pipes. These installations help purify the first flush of storm water before it discharges into city waterways. Ecological rehabilitation along the Chaoyang River through bio-engineering methods (such as in-stream solutions in the riverbed and green embankments) will improve the flood protection standard from 1-in-20 years between major flood events to 1-in-50 years. Trees will be planted alongside the riverbanks to create a greenbelt for new pedestrian and bicycle paths to be constructed. The design of the flood risk management measures is based on detailed hydraulic modeling (see Figure 6).

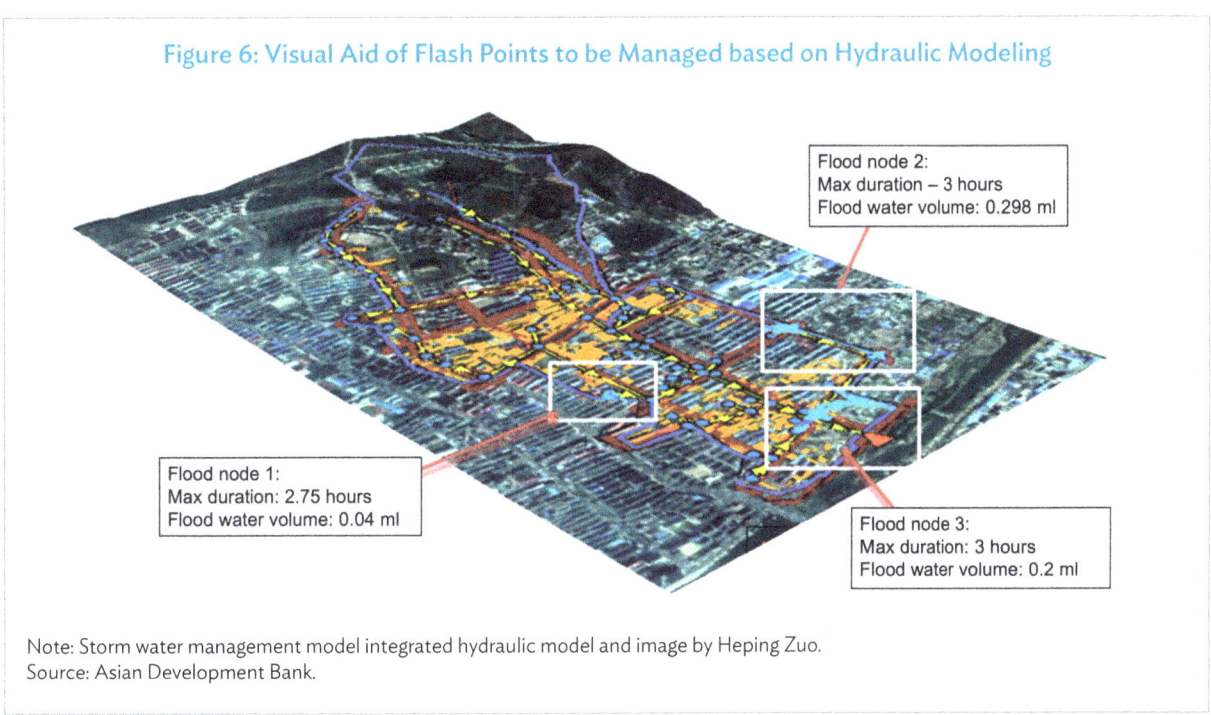

Figure 6: Visual Aid of Flash Points to be Managed based on Hydraulic Modeling

Note: Storm water management model integrated hydraulic model and image by Heping Zuo.
Source: Asian Development Bank.

Modern water supply. Updating Yanji's water system to the 21st Century with smart water meters, flow meters, and a system based on district metered areas that creates hydrologically isolated zones for more effective water monitoring, management, and leak detection and repair. The city's piped network, some of which is more than half a century old, will be replaced and others upgraded. The improvements will reduce the systems nonrevenue water rate from 46% to 37%, with further reductions expected to be possible during the project implementation and with improved planning and further investments.

Action plans and more knowledgeable staff. The vision driving the design of this project requires a concentrated yet comprehensive effort at master planning, action planning, implementation, and training across low carbon, transport-oriented urban development (see Figure 7 for a visual summary of the master plan and Box 2 for intended results). ADB is providing support for this knowledge work with the expectation that final plans will be approved by government. To emphasize the change in urban planning thinking in the city and other locations where the project will be promoted for its demonstration value, the following areas of study will be addressed: (i) planning and training under the project to create healthy, inclusive, livable cities (low carbon, transport-oriented development); (ii) urban climate change adaptation; (iii) traffic impact assessments, parking management, and nonmotorized transit networks; (iv) citywide hydraulic modeling and simulation with sponge city green infrastructure, open space systems, and HACAMP for healthy and age-inclusive city measures; and (v) smart city solutions (i.e. digital, cloud, automated, artificial intelligence, Internet of Things-based) for monitoring and managing city functions.

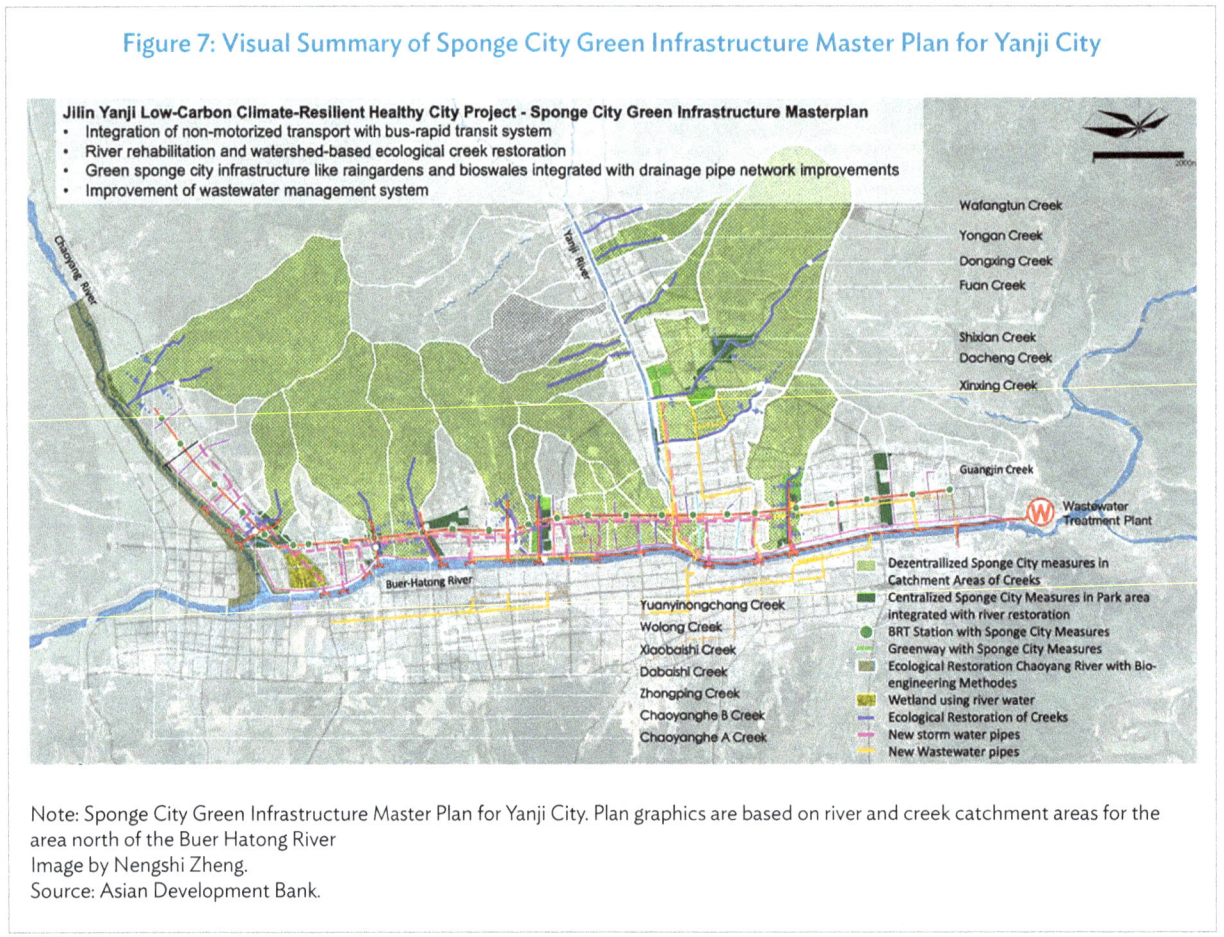

Figure 7: Visual Summary of Sponge City Green Infrastructure Master Plan for Yanji City

Note: Sponge City Green Infrastructure Master Plan for Yanji City. Plan graphics are based on river and creek catchment areas for the area north of the Buer Hatong River
Image by Nengshi Zheng.
Source: Asian Development Bank.

BOX 2

Summary of Intended Results for the Jilin Yanji Low Carbon Climate Resilient Healthy City Project

OUTCOME

Improved livability, low carbon development, climate resilience, and health in Yanji City. By 2028:
- Greenhouse gas emissions in Yanji City from transport sector reduced by 60,000 tons of carbon dioxide (tCO_2) per year..
- Mode share of public transport increased by 8%. 2017 baseline: 44%.
- Flood risk in urban catchment area of Chaoyang River reduced to 1-in-50 years. 2017 baseline: 1-in-20 years.
- Annual conservation of 4.8 million tons of drinking water achieved.

OUTPUT 1

Low carbon bus rapid transit (BRT) line integrated with nonmotorized transport infrastructure constructed. By 2027:

- BRT line of about 20 km and at least 25 stations constructed and equipped with wheelchair access, alarm buttons for women, priority seating, and safe lighting, especially for women.
- Fleet of at least 100 clean energy BRT buses procured; bus terminal building constructed.
- At least 30 km of pedestrian links to bus rapid transit (BRT) stations provided, including safe crossings and routes to schools and hospitals following universal design principles, with lighting to ensure safety for women.
- At least five plazas with landscaping and exercise equipment for all ages provided near BRT stations.
- Sidewalk parking prohibited in at least six locations along BRT corridor, 100 new parking spaces near BRT stations.
- At least 30 km of bicycle lanes along BRT corridor provided, linking to BRT stations, parking facilities at BRT stations.
- Priority seating installed in BRT buses for people with special needs (pregnant women, older people, and people with disabilities).
- At least one intelligent transport system command center established providing information services to operator users.
- At least 880 jobs created during project implementation and 350 jobs created during operation; at least 20% for local poor people and at least 20% for women during implementation and 30% for women during operation. 2017 baseline: 17% poor and 11% women in construction, and 25% women in operations.

OUTPUT 2

Constructed climate resilient flood risk management and sponge city green infrastructure.

- At least 4 km of river with improved flood risk, green embankments, and ecological low water level in-stream channel design and bicycle and pedestrian paths.
- At least 8,000 square meters of sponge city stormwater retention green space integrating physical activity areas for all ages and at least 43 km of drainage pipes and 40 km of wastewater pipes built.
- At least two end-of-storm-water pipe sedimentation tanks and reed-bed sand filters to clean first flush stormwater constructed. 2019 baseline: 0.
- At least 320 jobs created during project implementation, and 120 jobs created during operation, with at least 20% for local poor people and 20% for women during implementation and 30% for women during operation. 2017 baseline: 17% poor, 11% women in construction, 11% women in operation.

OUTPUT 3

Water supply system improved.

- At least 330 flow meters and 4,000 smart meters procured and installed.
- At least 32 km of leaking water supply pipes replaced.
- 483 jobs created during project implementation and 30 jobs created during operation, with at least 20% for poor people and 20% for women during implementation, and 30% for women during operation. 2017 baseline: 17% poor, and 11% women in construction and 25% women in operation.

OUTPUT 4

Capacity in low carbon, climate resilient, healthy city planning and infrastructure management developed (Baselines are 0 or not applicable).

- Action plans and guidelines which are inclusive and gender-sensitive prepared on low carbon, transport-oriented development, pedestrian and bicycle networks, urban climate change adaptation, citywide hydraulic model with sponge city green infrastructure, open space systems, and healthy city, are accepted by Yanji city government and shared with other cities in the People's Republic of China and other developing member countries.
- At least 50 staff (of which 40% are women) report improved knowledge on low carbon city planning and lifestyles, transport-oriented development, parking management, BRT advanced operations, urban climate change adaptation and community resilience, sponge city green infrastructure, healthy city, water safety, and nonrevenue water management.
- At least 30 government staff report improved capacity to assess water safety, develop effective mechanisms to reduce nonrevenue water, and operate geographic information systems and smart city solutions in Yanji.

[a] Yanji City Government. 2009. *Yanji City General Urban Master Development Plan (2009–2030)*. Yanji City.

Note: tCO_2 = ton of carbon dioxide.
Source: ADB. 2019. *Report and Recommendations to the President: Proposed Loan People's Republic of China: Jilin Yanji Low Carbon Climate Resilient Healthy City Project*.

Concerns for Sustainability and Impact

Implementation began in 2021, and some early evidence in the government's cooperation and commitment is providing reassuring signs that the integrated design will deliver the expected outcomes.

- Already, cross-sector cooperation among the administrative bureaus preparing and implementing the project has significantly improved, which is essential for successful implementation and operation. The communication and cooperation mechanism the project is using to bring all the implementing agencies and stakeholders together is holding regular meetings with the project director in the project management office and all involved implementing agencies. These meetings help coordinate engineering design, procurement and management of contractors and consultants and to monitor progress and discuss concerns and resolve issues.
- The project has been elevated to a top priority among the city's leaders, who consider it a beacon project as this is the first BRT line in the northeast region of the PRC. This is evident in the rapid response to all project related communications, local media coverage, its high status on the agendas of government meetings, and the effective and efficient operation of the project management office thanks to additional human resources.
- There have been cases of inappropriately designed BRT systems that led to overall traffic management inefficiencies and mismatches between design capacity and demand. To mitigate this risk and avoid overcapacity, the project team has been carefully studying demand and traffic in terms of realistic population forecasts. The road width of the corridor is sufficient to comfortably accommodate the BRT lanes and the remaining vehicular, bicycle, and pedestrian lanes and green landscape. Together,

- the integrated multimodal transport, nonmotorized transport, and green sponge city infrastructure and landscape improvements will make the city more pedestrian friendly.
- The experience from the PRC's sponge city program has seen cases where fragmented investments have not reduced flooding and the selection of green space construction and plant selection proved hard to maintain. Learning from these early lessons, the project analysis and design teams developed a more comprehensive catchment-based approach and integrated green and gray infrastructure system design. The prioritization of green infrastructure as part of project financing focused on areas most affected by flooding.

Notes on Replication

In this project, the project team leader and staff identified the following lessons. These are worth considering by other project team leaders as they analyze development problems and face challenges designing innovative projects.

- Secure effective government engagement through close collaboration and communication. A close client relationship comes from listening to how clients understand their city's development challenges. Be sure to understand their plans. Discuss ideas for project design that deliver optimal benefits with the time and funds available while also addressing key challenges of social and economic development and inclusion, service provision, climate change, and environmental pollution.
- Consultants' communication skills are as important as their technical excellence. A project benefits exponentially from a consultant who is both technically sound and able to effectively explain new and complex ideas to government agencies, political leaders, local experts and engineers and other team members who need to adapt their own technical knowledge to contribute to integrating novel ideas into a project.
- Be ready for challenges from political change. Ideas and plans will need to be re-explained to develop renewed political support and ownership of a project when there are changes in government leadership.
- Consider planners and other generalists as 'integration specialists' and an added human resource to ADB's sector specialists.
- Developing member countries and cities where planning systems are weak should have mission leaders who can envision opportunities and engage in effective consultations with government on integrating investments for greater synergies and co-benefits.
- Proposing and implementing nature-based solutions using ecosystem services in green infrastructure remains challenging as governments, engineers and contractors still favor gray over green infrastructure. Acceptance and overcoming inertia comes from showing evidence from successful projects and methods and quantifying economic benefits. It is important to improve both technical and general project design and appraisal methodologies.
- Seize opportunities for advanced, comprehensive planning.

Advice on Innovation

Rau offers the following advice for other mission leaders facing challenges that call for innovative thinking.

- Be confident to move outside the comfort zone of your own expertise. Moderate a process that allows ideas to emerge, engage with, listen to, trust, gently push and elevate your experts, and create a productive environment that motivates all to excel to create an impactful project together.
- Carefully study the context and situation of a place and its challenges and get a good understanding of the opportunities for development, and then develop a vision and ideas and push in various directions until a project emerges that's within the realm of possibility.
- Work with local officials, stakeholders and people to create broad project ownership and engage in consultation and make these local experts and beneficiaries part of the innovations. Help them articulate the big vision and principles of a project, then they will be champions and run with it.

Learn More

- Read: https://www.adb.org/projects/50322-002/main
- See case study in Chapter 5E: https://www.adb.org/publications/creating-livable-asian-cities
- See presentation on healthy and age-friendly cities: https://events.development.asia/materials/20200514/healthy-and-age-friendly-cities-peoples-republic-china
- See presentation on nature-based solutions and sponge cities: https://events.development.asia/materials/20210715/sponge-cities-people-s-republic-china-evolution-adb-support

Contact: **Stefan Rau,**
Senior Urban Development Specialist
srau@adb.org

VIET NAM

The Binh Duong Water Treatment Expansion Project

A First in Viet Nam's Water Sector: Utility Transitions to Nonsovereign Lending

with Won Myong Hong and Satoshi Ishii

Project Name	Binh Duong Water Treatment Expansion Project
Project Location	Binh Duong Province in Viet Nam
ADB Team	Private Sector Infrastructure Finance 2, Southeast Asia Urban Development and Water
Sector	Urban water supply
Year Approved	2020 (October)
Borrower	Binh Duong Water Environment Joint Stock Company
Loan Amount	$8 million
Grant Amount	$500,000
Financial Modalities	Nonsovereign, London Inter-Bank Offered Rate; LIBOR-based regular loan from ordinary capital resources Co-financing loan from Japan International Cooperation Agency Technical assistance grant from the Republic of Korea e-Asia and Knowledge Partnership Fund
Project Scope	Support Viet Nam's private water operators with its first nonsovereign loan to expand water treatment capacity by 100 million liters daily
Design Team Leader(s)	Won Myong Hong, Senior Investment Specialist for the Private Sector Infrastructure Finance Division 2 Satoshi Ishii, Unit Head, Project Administration for Viet Nam Resident Mission
Current Project Officer	Kiron Nath, Senior Investment Specialist, Portfolio Management Division

The Development Need

Binh Duong is one of Viet Nam's fastest developing provinces, which explains why 2016–2019 experienced annual water demand increases of 16%–20%. By 2021, water demand was expected to exceed the production capacity of the province's private water operator, Binh Duong Water Environment Joint Stock Company (BIWASE). BIWASE needed to expand its water treatment capacity by 100,000 cubic meters per day (m^3/day) and install additional water intake pumps and 9 kilometers of raw water transmission pipes. The development seemed to warrant a typical water supply project, but the financing became the country's first nonsovereign loan to the water sector.

> The development need may seem to warrant a typical water supply project, but the financing was far from typical. It became a first.
>
> —Won Myong Hong, Senior Investment Specialist for the Private Sector Infrastructure Finance Division 2

Development Challenges

BIWASE had benefited from ADB sovereign financing in the past. When it corporatized, it no longer qualified for sovereign lending. Although its success as a relatively new privatized water operator had quickly graduated the utility to the next rung of nonsovereign loans, BIWASE did not have the creditworthiness to qualify for competitive long-term financing from private investors.

A first for ADB, Viet Nam. A One ADB team prepared the bank's first nonsovereign loan in Viet Nam's water sector. The investment enabled Binh Duong Water Environment Joint Stock Company to expand the capacity of the Tan Hiep Water Treatment Plant by 100,000 cubic meters per day, for a total daily production of 600,000 cubic meters (photo provided by BIWASE).

Project-based Solutions

ADB project staff recognized an opportunity to transition BIWASE to ADB's nonsovereign lending operations to provide it with the necessary financing to expand its production capacity and meet future demand while also improving its creditworthiness for future long-term commercial financing.

The Risks

ADB's Private Sector Operations Department (PSOD) had yet to take on a client in the water sector in Viet Nam or the Greater Mekong Subregion (GMS) because of weak regulations that expose both borrower and lender to financial instability and weak accountability.

"PSOD has always been keen on investing in the water sector, but there are inherent challenges," said Won Myong Hong, Senior Investment Specialist for the Private Sector Infrastructure Finance Division 2. "Given the lack of clear regulatory frameworks, the water sector in Viet Nam is not yet considered fertile ground for private sector investment."

In 2007, the Viet Nam government began corporatizing provincial water operators and other government owned utilities and companies and converting them to publicly owned joint stock companies by selling shares to private investors and on the stock exchange to integrate them into the global market and attract foreign investment. However, the necessary financial and institutional reforms to attract long-term commercial financing in the water sector have not yet materialized. For example, the central government and provincial line agency roles, policies, and regulations are misaligned. This results in fragmentation and weak oversight of water operators, who are left to their own devices to balance business decisions between shareholder expectations and equitable, affordable public service. Water utilities also have no or only weak legally enforceable contracts with their respective provincial governments, who approve water tariffs. Reducing the provincial government's share of ownership in water utilities and transferring financial responsibility could expose the utility to financial unsustainability, especially absent any clear service agreement between the provincial government and the utility to secure safe and sustainable public services.

BIWASE was a borderline case for PSOD, although it has been one of Viet Nam's strongest provincial urban-based water operators. As a development bank, ADB is in a position to take a high-potential agency and make it viable for future investors who would not be amenable to such risks at present. To make this happen, BIWASE needed to adopt international financial reporting standards, a long-term corporate business strategy, and a business plan that considered a changing market environment and climate risks into its operations.

BIWASE is one of the largest water utilities in Viet Nam. It is 80% owned by nongovernment shareholders and listed on the stock exchange. It has benefited from ADB's sovereign (public) loan supports approved in 2001 and 2012. With the end of the sovereign water sector investment program approaching, Satoshi Ishii, former Principal Urban Development Specialist for Southeast Asia Department (SERD) and presently the Unit Head for project administration for the Viet Nam Resident Mission, said his team started looking for commercial financing for BIWASE in 2019 as the government could no longer guarantee loans for BIWASE. On ADB's financing ladder, BIWASE was ready to graduate to the next rung of nonsovereign loans.

"If PSOD was going to do a project in the Viet Nam water sector for the first time, it would need an ideal client," Hong said.

The Opportunities

A successful loan negotiation and project implementation with BIWASE would:

- Signal to commercial banks and foreign investors that BIWASE is a financially viable, creditworthy entity.
- Stimulate growth through a new commercial financing stream for viable medium-sized water operators in Viet Nam.
- Enable PSOD and other international development finance institutions to access the urban water market in Viet Nam and the GMS.

Utilities like BIWASE must raise capital, either through local commercial banks or bond issues. BIWASE could have secured cheaper loans from a commercial bank but borrowing from ADB's nonsovereign lending program offered BIWASE added credibility.

> It did not take much time for us to come out of our comfort zones. SERD brought our best client to PSOD.
>
> — Satoshi Ishii, Unit Head, Project Administration for Viet Nam Resident Mission, Southeast Asia Department

Historically, PSOD would not prioritize companies like BIWASE that have relatively brief histories, smaller revenue potential, and lower financing needs than national or multinational companies. In 2020, however, ADB adopted a key performance indicator aimed at increasing the *number* of private sector loans over the *amount* of private sector loans. This strategic corporate shift expanded opportunities between ADB and companies like BIWASE. Still, BIWASE would need innovative and complex financing structures and agreements to ensure it would have the necessary accountability, integrity, and creditworthiness in place or in progress. Meanwhile, SERD and BIWASE looked for an opportunity to demonstrate new financing approaches for the water sector in Viet Nam.

"It was a matter of good timing that PSOD's expanding interests, SERD's long-term sector strategy, and BIWASE's evolving corporate interests came together when they did," Ishii said. "It did not take much time for us to come out of our comfort zones. SERD brought their best client to PSOD. If this couldn't work, ADB would not be able to support the transitioning water sector in Viet Nam"

Innovations and Firsts

- The Binh Duong Water Treatment Expansion Project would be ADB's first nonsovereign loan to a urban water supply operator in Viet Nam and the GMS.
- By servicing BIWASE's financing needs, ADB could also improve the corporate culture within BIWASE for women and set a new standard.

Investments move the water. A One ADB team of Southeast Asia Department and Private Sector Operations Department helped one of Viet Nam's best water providers, Binh Duong Water Environment Joint Stock Company, access the country's first multilateral nonsovereign loan to the sector. The loan enabled BIWASE to expand its system with infrastructure like this 1,500-millimeter raw pipeline (photo provided by BIWASE).

BIWASE initially proposed a $50 million loan to increase its production capacity by 100,000 m³/day and expand its network to unconnected households. During the first joint meeting between BIWASE management, the PSOD team and the SERD team, PSOD's loan terms were initially not well received by BIWASE management. They were used to ADB's sovereign loan terms, but BIWASE no longer qualified for those loans.

"They pushed back strongly," Hong said, "and wanted more time to think about the terms and negotiate them." Ishii recalls being surprised by PSOD's approach, which sent a clear message to the client on pricing, which is aligned with the market in a way to not undercut other commercial lenders. The terms were firm. Hong explained that, "We needed to be quite direct from the beginning to set the right expectations. We had that experience already."

There was an incentive for BIWASE and ADB to work together. BIWASE would be ADB's first water utility in Viet Nam and the GMS to secure its nonsovereign loan. "It becomes part of BIWASE's brand and helps them get better lending terms and investor access, in addition to technical assistance grant support of course" Ishii said.

Because SERD had a good rapport with and knowledge of BIWASE from previous projects, Ishii said they were able to act as a mediator to explain and advise both sides. "SERD's existing relationship and understanding of BIWASE greatly helped in facilitating the commercial discussions and helped get BIWASE over the line," Hong said.

To make the partnership possible, BIWASE reduced the loan proposal to $16 million by contributing more from its own capital resources. ADB also introduced co-financing from Japan International Cooperation Agency (JICA), which had previous investment experience with BIWASE. "Everyone wanted to make the deal work," Hong said.

ADB's project financing is relatively small compared to the traditional sovereign lending water supply expansion project.

We were a little skeptical, but we took on the project … We liked the smaller size of the loan because we are new to the sector.

— Won Myong Hong, Senior Investment Specialist for the Private Sector Infrastructure Finance Division 2

The burden of project preparation for PSOD operations is typically on the client, unlike ADB's sovereign operations that support government clients financially and technically to prepare the project documents required for loan processing. In this case, SERD played an intermediary role to ensure BIWASE's documentation was up to PSOD standards. SERD used staff consultants and technical assistance budgets to help BIWASE.

Both Ishii and Hong say they were surprised by how well the PSOD and SERD staff worked together as a single team. They had a broad scope of work to accomplish. PSOD staff handled the financial and legal discussions while the SERD staff handled the sector, social and environmental due diligence tasks. The gender action plan was the work of PSOD's gender team.

"This was truly a One ADB approach because it needed both sides to make this happen," Ishii said.

Project Basics

ADB's financing directly supports the expansion of BIWASE water treatment plant capacity by 100 million liters per day (MLD) or 100,000 m³/day. A technical assistance grant is supporting improvements in BIWASE's capacity for financial management and business planning, and securing agreements between BIWASE and the government on legal provisions for water supply services.[3] The project is also supporting institutional changes within BIWASE's that will result in improved credit worthiness and greater gender inclusiveness. These include changes in workplace gender norms that will improve the balance between employees' personal and professional time and responsibilities (work-life balance). Ultimately, BIWASE should be more attractive to private investors after the project (Box 3).

---

[3] These provisions are based on Article 31 of the Decree 117 on Clean Water Production, Supply, and Consumption as well as amendment number 126. UN Environment Programme and Law and Environment Assistance Platform. https://leap.unep.org/countries/vn/national-legislation/decree-no-1172007nd-cp-clean-water-production-supply-and.

BOX 3

Summary of Intended Results for Viet Nam: The Binh Duong Water Treatment Expansion Project

OUTCOME

Residents of Binh Duong Province are assured of adequate and reliable potable water. By 2025.
- 72,000 households connected to Binh Duong Water Environment Joint Stock Company (BIWASE) water supply system for the first time.
- BIWASE increases its water supply production by 32.85 million cubic meters per year (m^3/year).

OUTPUT 1

The existing Tan Hiep water treatment plant is expanded. By 2023:
- The Tan Hiep plant is producing an additional 100,000 cubic meters per day (m^3/day).
- Nine kilometers of new raw transmission pipes are installed to enable increased production at the Tan Hiep plant.

OUTPUT 2

BIWASE's creditworthiness and institutional capacity is enhanced. By 2023:
- At least 10 staff of BIWASE's finance department (50% women) gain enhanced skills and knowledge on IFRS reporting.
- Draft a water service agreement with performance indicators as a step toward greater contractual accountability between BIWASE and the Binh Duong Provincial People's Committee.

OUTPUT 3

BIWASE demonstrates greater commitment to the women's workforce. By 2023:
- Women will be hired for at least 10 of the 80 jobs available during the project construction phase.
- BIWASE will increase the proportion of women in management to 13.
- BIWASE will develop and implement a gender policy by 2021 that aims to hire, retain, and promote women.

OUTPUT 4

Initiate gender norm change within BIWASE work-life balance. By 2023:
- Given the lessons and experiences of the Coronavirus disease (COVID-19) crisis for workers managing professional and family needs, BIWASE will develop and implement a policy by 2021 that provides employees with flexible work arrangements.

Source: ADB. 2020. *FAST Report, Loan and Administration of Technical Assistance Grant, Binh Duong Water Environment Joint Stock Company, Binh Duong Water Treatment Expansion Project (Viet Nam)*. Manila.

Notes on Replication

The experience of processing the Binh Duong project has resulted in some widely applicable lessons for ADB in general and, more specifically, for project officers considering proposing a project for PSOD consideration.

The Right Corporate Strategy Can Incentivize Innovation.
The case of Binh Duong demonstrates the power of the right corporate strategy to inspire innovation, healthy risk-taking involved in innovating, and determination to make the innovation work. By ADB adopting a key performance indicator (KPI) on the number of PSOD processed loans, PSOD was able to reconsider clients who had previously not been as 'ideal' as other 'big potential' clients. Part of the process of choosing clients is about allocating limited staff resources efficiently. Now, with the internal emphasis on the number of loans rather than the value of loans, PSOD has an incentive to broaden its scope of interest. "Had the KPIs not changed, BIWASE would not have been attractive to PSOD," Ishii said. "The KPI enabled PSOD and SERD to think innovatively about who it does business with and how to grow its portfolio but always in ways that bring the same development benefits to Asia and the Pacific."

Co-financing Can Make the Investment Graduation More Affordable for Smaller Clients.
BIWASE had initially asked for $50 million, but given PSOD's risk appetite, it required a co-financing partner to meet the client's need. Similarly with ADB, BIWASE had experience with JICA, so its management felt comfortable with ADB's suggestion to involve JICA as a strategy to take advantage of ADB's nonsovereign loan but minimize the loan amount. JICA relied on ADB's due diligence and offered to lend an amount equal to ADB.

Non-refundable Technical Assistance Grants May Be Necessary to Graduate Clients from Sovereign to Nonsovereign Lending Projects.
The BIWASE project secured a $500,000 non-refundable technical assistance grant from the Republic of Korea e-Asia and Knowledge Partnership Fund. A non-refundable technical assistance grant attached to the loan is unusual for private sector loans. BIWASE is in a transition state to graduate from sovereign loan support to more commercial finance. "We were determined to foster our long-term partnership with BIWASE and grow together," Ishii said. "This kind of technical assistance may be needed in the future for these smaller potential clients for PSOD. Urban water supply is a big market, and ADB can offer a combination of products to strengthen this middle tier in graduating from sovereign loans to fully commercial loans."

Ishii also advocates for the non-refundable technical assistance grant for certain nonsovereign projects because of its value-added development benefits. "ADB prides itself on being honest brokers," he said. "Our selling point is we offer credibility for international investors and we bring technical assistance money to continue capacity development. We support the borrower and not just financially. Through this, we support the entire sector and so the country."

Newly Privatized Clients Need a Transition in Mindset.
Former government owned companies and utilities like BIWASE that demonstrate potential will need support beyond transitioning to market-oriented, investor-friendly processes and policies. The staff and workplace culture will need support in transitioning from a government to a corporate mindset. This was evident from initial discussions with private lenders, as BIWASE still expected the rates and conditions of its previous sovereign loans. The project that was designed and approved for BIWASE included institutional capacity development to align workplace culture with development values such as social equity and inclusion, operational efficiency and productivity

Pay Close Attention to Securities Risks.
BIWASE had to clearly delineate its securities for the project. The local banks and BIWASE had not been paying attention to the security risks, as they were overlapping. Utilities and banks need to fix overlapping securities for multilaterals and international lenders to do business with them. BIWASE has had to go back to their banks and fix the overlapping securities, which served as an opportunity for developing their capacity.

> The sovereign operations teams can help make some of these transactions possible for PSOD. We know the sectors, the clients, and the risks.
>
> — Satoshi Ishii, Unit Head, Project Administration for Viet Nam Resident Mission

Nonsovereign lending can influence and grow more equitable corporate cultures.
ADB's nonsovereign lending added value by introducing more progressive benchmarks and standards for gender development that will positively affect social change within the workplace cultures of developing member countries. BIWASE already had a good understanding of ADB's expectations to promote gender equality from its experience with ADB sovereign loans. For the nonsovereign loan preparation, the PSOD gender team found that BIWASE had already made significant progress in promoting gender equality through the previous sovereign loan. The ADB team decided on more innovative and progressive indicators for BIWASE to advance gender equality in the company even further. BIWASE agreed to:

- Increase the proportion of women in management from eight in 2019 to 13.
- Develop and implement a gender policy that would lead to more women being hired, retained and promoted by 2021.
- Develop and implement a flexible work arrangement policy by 2021 based on the experience and lessons from the Coronavirus disease (COVID-19) crisis.

"PSOD really thought innovatively with the project and introduced a new level of gender development indicators for BIWASE," Ishii said.

The PSOD gender specialist had suggested a range of potential gender indicators to BIWASE, and they chose those indicators they were most comfortable with adopting.

Notes on the One ADB Experience

PSOD and sovereign operational staff do not have a long history of working closely together. "We haven't had much chance to either," Ishii said. "But with the kind of transaction like BIWASE, we have a chance to understand each other's work."

The experience of helping both BIWASE and PSOD in processing the project demonstrated the value of both sovereign and nonsovereign teams, even if the lending is purely nonsovereign.

"The sovereign operations teams can help make some of these transactions possible for PSOD. We know the sectors, the clients, and the risks," Ishii said. "On PSOD's side, they have choices in clients, so they can be more selective, systematic, and direct. The sovereign side has to rely on PSOD's judgment. They have their own expertise and we (the sovereign side) need to understand how PSOD operations work."

Learn More

Read: https://www.adb.org/projects/54074-001/main

Contact: **Won Myong Hong,**
Senior Investment Specialist
Private Sector Infrastructure Finance Division 2
whong@adb.org

Satoshi Ishii,
Unit Head, Project Administration
Viet Nam Resident Mission
sishii@adb.org

Kiron Nath,
Senior Investment Specialist
Portfolio Management Division
knath@adb.org

THE PEOPLE'S REPUBLIC OF CHINA

Climate Resilient and Smart Urban Water Infrastructure Project

Nonsovereign PRC Loan Demonstrates Broad Integration of Smart Water Technologies

with Yihong Wang, Anqian Huang, Zhijia Rao, and Jinqiang Chen

Project Name	Climate-Resilient and Smart Urban Water Infrastructure Project
Project Location	Shenzhen and smaller, less developed cities across the People's Republic of China
ADB Team	East Asia Department, Private Sector Operations Department
Sector	Urban sewerage, urban water supply, other urban services
Year Approved	2020 (November)
Borrower	Shenzhen Water (Group) Co., Ltd. and Shenzhen Water and Environment Investment Group Co., Ltd.
Loan Amount	$200 million
Financial Modalities	Corporate loan, OCR: $200 million
Project Scope	To support Shenzhen Water Group Company's investment in multiple water supply and wastewater treatment facilities with smart water technologies and climate- and disaster-resilient urban water infrastructure in Shenzhen and smaller cities in the People's Republic of China (PRC).
Design Team Leader(s)	Jinqiang Chen, Urban Specialist, EAPF, EARD Anqian Huang, Senior Financial Sector Specialist, EAPF, EARD Zhijia Rao, Senior Investment Officer, Infrastructure Finance Division 2, Private Sector Operations Department Yihong Wang, Senior Investment Officer, PRC Resident Mission, EARD

The Development Need

Third and fourth tier cities in the People's Republic of China (PRC) need to upgrade their water supply and sewerage systems with smart water solutions to reduce nonrevenue water, optimize energy efficiency, enhance service qualities, and strengthen long-term operations and maintenance of the systems. These cities also need infrastructure that can manage the seasonal fluxes in rainfall.

The Development Challenges

Many PRC cities face a deluge of challenges related to water (Figure 8), Water availability, water quality, and increasing demand from urbanization represent the services side of the country's water distress, while the other comes from climate change. New seasonal fluctuations in rainfall and intensifying extreme rains are overwhelming drainage and sewerage infrastructure, causing increased risks and urban floods. Implementing sweeping changes at an economic scale in separate cities is a challenge.

Figure 8: Water Distress in the People's Republic of China

Per capita water resources are about one-quarter of the global average[a]

25% of water bodies do not meet minimum drinking water quality standards[b]

Rapidly increasing urban water demand means the country needs a 20% greater total water supply than in 2014[c]

[a] National Bureau of Statistics of China. National Database. http://data.stats.gov.cn (accessed 6 June 2020).
[b] Government of the People's Republic of China, Ministry of Ecology and Environment. 2020. Report on the State of Environment in China 2019. Beijing.
[c] Asian Development Bank (ADB). 2018. Managing Water Resources for Sustainable Socioeconomic Development: A Country Water Assessment for the People's Republic of China. Manila.

Source: Asian Development Bank.

Project-based Solutions

The government is promoting the sponge city approach and smart water technology as solutions for the country's vexing water challenges. (Box 4). Rolling these out in smaller cities needs an economic scale. The PRC has over 100 cities with 1 million people or more. To achieve an economy of scale would require private sector participation and research, development, and demonstration for implementation in smaller cities. Under the sovereign window, ADB approved its first sponge city pilot in 2017 in Pingxiang in Jiangxi Province and has since approved a second sponge city loan project in Yanji in Jilin Province (see case study on Jilin Yanji Sponge City Project). To implement the concepts of a sponge city and smart water in smaller cities, private sector investments and operational know-how are important.

BOX 4

Sponge City and Smart Water Defined

A sponge city has a water infrastructure system designed to act like a sponge and soak up urban runoff: It absorbs, stores, filters, purifies, and slowly releases urban runoff. The sponge city approach uses a mix of green and grey infrastructure. Strategic parks and green spaces, for example, counter the nonporous surfaces that create flood hazards in cities. A sponge city provides safer drainage, prevents flooding, offers opportunities to reuse rainwater, and protects the environment.

Smart water solutions use artificial intelligence, information communication technology (ICT) and the Internet of Things (IoT) to improve water quality and supply, reduce leaks, enhance wastewater treatment and reuse, support monitoring and evaluation, improve customer service, and reduce energy consumption.

Source: The authors.

Innovations and Firsts

- Bundle smaller investments to make subprojects in separate cities cost effective.
- Mobilize private sector investments in urban resilience, especially with water infrastructure.
- Transform water supply and wastewater utilities into water and environmental management providers.
- Integrate smart water technologies into all subprojects (sponge city, water and wastewater subprojects).

ADB's sovereign operations team in its East Asia Department (EARD) was looking to develop the sector by joining forces with ADB's nonsovereign staff in the Private Sector Operations Department (PSOD). "It was the first joint EARD-PSOD nonsovereign project, so we were very careful to pick the right project sponsor, one that was operationally and financially strong and shares ADB's development vision. It was a learning process because it was one of the earlier One ADB projects," said Yihong Wang, Senior Investment Officer, PRC Resident Mission, EARD.

The One ADB team identified its ideal client as Shenzhen Water (Group) Co., Ltd. (SZWG) during an ADB knowledge and support technical assistance project with the government of the PRC. Established in 2001, SZWG is a leading water utility in the PRC. Shenzhen Water and Environment Investment Group Co., Ltd. is an investment platform for SZWG operations outside Shenzhen. Shenzhen was one of the first cities in the PRC to integrate water supply and sewerage services. As of 2019, SZWG managed 129 water supply and wastewater treatment facilities, collectively serving over 30 million people across 22 cities in the PRC.

SZWG has reduced nonrevenue water levels in Shenzhen to less than 10% by deploying smart water technologies. It has also participated in ADB knowledge forums on water operations and climate resilience. Entering the urban green infrastructure space opens up the urban water utility's mandate.

> It was the first joint EARD-PSOD nonsovereign project, so we were very careful to pick the right project sponsor, one that was operationally and financially strong and shares ADB's development vision.
>
> — Yihong Wang, Senior Investment Officer, PRC Resident Mission, EARD

It took some time to convince municipalities to support SZWG's investments in green infrastructure and pursue sponge city approaches outside the government's pilot program. In contrast, gray infrastructure (pipes, treatment plants, the materials of hard infrastructure) has been the traditional purview of utilities. So EARD and PSOD worked together with the SZWG to develop a project demonstrating private sector participation in sponge city and smart technology applications.

Advocating for Innovation

The project took three years from concept to approval and conducted the standard due diligence on nonsovereign clients. ADB and the Shenzhen Municipal Government supported SZWG's efforts to obtain a shadow credit rating from Standard & Poor's, which improved its credit rating in ADB's pricing tools. In addition, the Water Sector Group of the Sustainable Development and Climate Change Department (SDCC) advised the project team on climate resilient and smart water techniques and technologies. The additional reviews helped SZWG level up its digitization plan.

 "This project was really the result of both sides working together. PSOD looked at the client and their pipeline and tried to develop a financing approach. We [PSOD] traditionally rely on a client's advice," said Zhijia Rao, Senior Investment Officer, Infrastructure Finance Division 2, PSOD. "But working with the sovereign side, they brought up the questions for the technical side of things."

> The ADB assistance helps SZWG develop a strong gender action plan to better empower women in recruitment, retention, and promotion… The project also looks into knowledge development of climate resilience for women.
>
> — Anqian Huang, Senior Financial Sector Specialist, EAPF, EARD

Without ADB support, SZWG would have had to raise financing for each project city through local branches of commercial banks. Long-term financing remains scarce for the climate resilient and smart urban water sector, which are new to commercial banks. ADB links the cluster of projects with broader financing, including international financial institutions. ADB's facility intends to catalyze private sector resources through various co-financing arrangements during project implementation.

Broader financing for smaller cities. Chizhou is one of 22 cities in the People's Republic of China with water supply and wastewater facilities privately managed by Shenzhen Water (Group) Co., Ltd. (SZWG). ADB's financing enables SZWG to upgrade clusters of cities with smart water and sponge city solutions but under one broad financing package, a first for ADB that promises good demonstration value (photo provided by SZWG).

The project also demonstrates private-public participation in the sector. SZWG will create a subproject corporation (a special purpose vehicle) in each project city to segregate the risks. "It does develop the public-private partnership through the contract with the city government. The ring-fence through concession rights," said Yihong Wang, Senior Investment Officer, PRC Resident Mission (PRCM), EARD.

With the prestige of ADB financing, SZWG was in an influential position to demonstrate progressive gender policies to the corporate world.

"We found that SZWG was a good candidate for piloting corporate gender mainstreaming. The ADB assistance helps SZWG develop a strong gender action plan to recruit, retain, promote, and empower women, while enhancing their core technical capacities," said Anqian Huang, Senior Financial Sector Specialist, EAPF, EARD. "The project also looks into knowledge development of climate resilience for women."

Project Basics

The sector knowledge of EARD and SDCC combined with PSOD's transaction expertise and skills has provided SZWG with a single framework for designing and promoting a project that incorporates sponge city development with smart water technology applications and greater gender inclusion.

Women figure prominently in the design of the Climate Resilient and Smart Water Project (Box 5). The first of the project's three main outputs are infrastructure-driven and focus on constructing or rehabilitating urban water systems for greater climate resilience and smart technology systems.

Aside from the hard infrastructure elements, the project showcases ADB's value addition for work that advances the country's understanding of the unique challenges women face in urban and corporate environments. The second output supports project impact monitoring that will identify how sponge city and smart water technology applications can contribute to women's resilience to climate change and disasters. Finally, the project supports a forum for disseminating this knowledge to influence future sponge city and smart water project designs (see Box 5 for intended results).

The third project output supports the project company, SZWG, in fostering a more gender-inclusive corporate environment through policy changes and added employee benefits. More than positively affecting this one company and its subsidiaries, SZWG demonstrates a new HR standard for gender inclusiveness for water service providers and other industries.

BOX 5

Summary of Intended Results for the Climate Resilient and Smart Urban Water Infrastructure Project in the People's Republic of China

OUTCOME

Expanded climate resilient and smart urban water management. By 2026:
- At least $40 million in equivalent capital expenditures invested for flood mitigation.
- At least 2 million more people benefiting from improved urban water services in urban areas.
- Increase of about 100 million cubic meters per year (m^3/year) of water.
- Increase of about 40 million cubic meters per year (m^3/year) of treated wastewater.
- At least 10 women employees promoted to mid-level or high-level management positions at SZWG. 2019 baseline: 3.

OUTPUT 1

New and rehabilitated climate resilient and smart urban water systems in selected cities. By 2025:
- At least one sponge city subproject with reduced flood risk implemented.
- Water supply capacity using smart water technology added or improved by about 400,000 cubic meters per day (m³/day).
- Wastewater treatment capacity using smart water technology added or improved by about 200,000 cubic meters per day (m³/day).

OUTPUT 2

Knowledge of sponge city and smart water technology application that promotes increased resilience of women to climate change and disasters increased. By 2023:
- Produce at least one knowledge product on how sponge city and smart water technologies promote increased resilience of women to climate change and disasters.
- At least 50 industry players and other participants (at least 30% women) participate in at least one knowledge sharing event and gain improved understanding on how to construct sponge cities and apply smart water technologies.

OUTPUT 3

Improved gender inclusiveness at SZWG. By 2023:
- A human resources policy prepared for SZWG that aims to increase the proportion of women staff recruited, retained, and promoted. 2019 baseline: current HR policy does not have specific terms to increase proportion of women staff recruited, retained, and promoted.
- At least 35% of staff in professional training for career advancement are women. 2019 baseline: 30%.

Note: SZWG = Shenzhen Water (Group) Co., Ltd.
Source: ADB. 2021. *Report and Recommendations to the President: Proposed Loan for Climate Resilient and Smart Urban Water Infrastructure Project (People's Republic of China)*.

Notes on Replication

Implementation lessons and results from the broad, integrated application of smart water technologies provides demonstration value for the industry in the PRC but also regionally and globally. The project supports knowledge dissemination of results that may be instrumental in policy dialogues and advocating for wider uptake of smart technologies in PRC cities with private sector participation.

Learn More

Read: https://www.adb.org/projects/52090-001/main

Contact: **Jinqiang Chen,**
Urban Specialist, EAPF, EARD,
jchen@adb.org

Zhijia Rao,
Senior Investment Officer, Infrastructure Finance Division 2,
Private Sector Operations Department,
zrao@adb.org

INDIA

Inclusive, Resilient, Sustainable Housing for Urban Poor Sector Project in Tamil Nadu, India

Beyond Slum Upgrades: How Affordable Housing Projects Build Resilient, Thriving Households

with Ricardo Carlos Barba

Project Name	Inclusive, Resilient and Sustainable Housing for Urban Poor Sector Project in Tamil Nadu
Project Location	State of Tamil Nadu, India
ADB Team	South Asia Urban and Water Division
Sector	Urban housing
Year Approved	2021
Borrower	Government of Tamil Nadu, India
Loan Amount	$150 million
Grant Amount	$1.5 million (Technical Assistance Special Fund)
Financial Modalities	Ordinary capital resources
Project Scope	The project promotes access to inclusive, resilient, and sustainable housing and urban development in Tamil Nadu by supporting the state in (i) relocating vulnerable communities from climate hazard-prone areas; (ii) providing affordable, well-maintained housing for low-income urban households and migrant workers; and (iii) supporting the state in regional development planning.
Design Team Leader(s)	Ricardo Carlos Barba, Principal Safeguards Specialist Sourav Majumder, Senior Project Officer (Urban), India Resident Mission (current project officer)
Executing Agency	Housing and Urban Development Department and the Tamil Nadu Slum Clearance Board, Government of Tamil Nadu

The Development Need

Low-income households and migrant workers need safe, affordable, well-maintained housing connected to urban services and close to employment and income opportunities.

Core Development Challenges

- Insufficiently managed rapid urbanization and in-migration.
- Urban infrastructure and public services cannot meet demand.
- Acute shortage of housing, an exclusive problem for low-income households and migrant workers.
- Low-income settlements in hazard-prone areas.
- The housing gap is too wide for the state government, already a major housing provider.

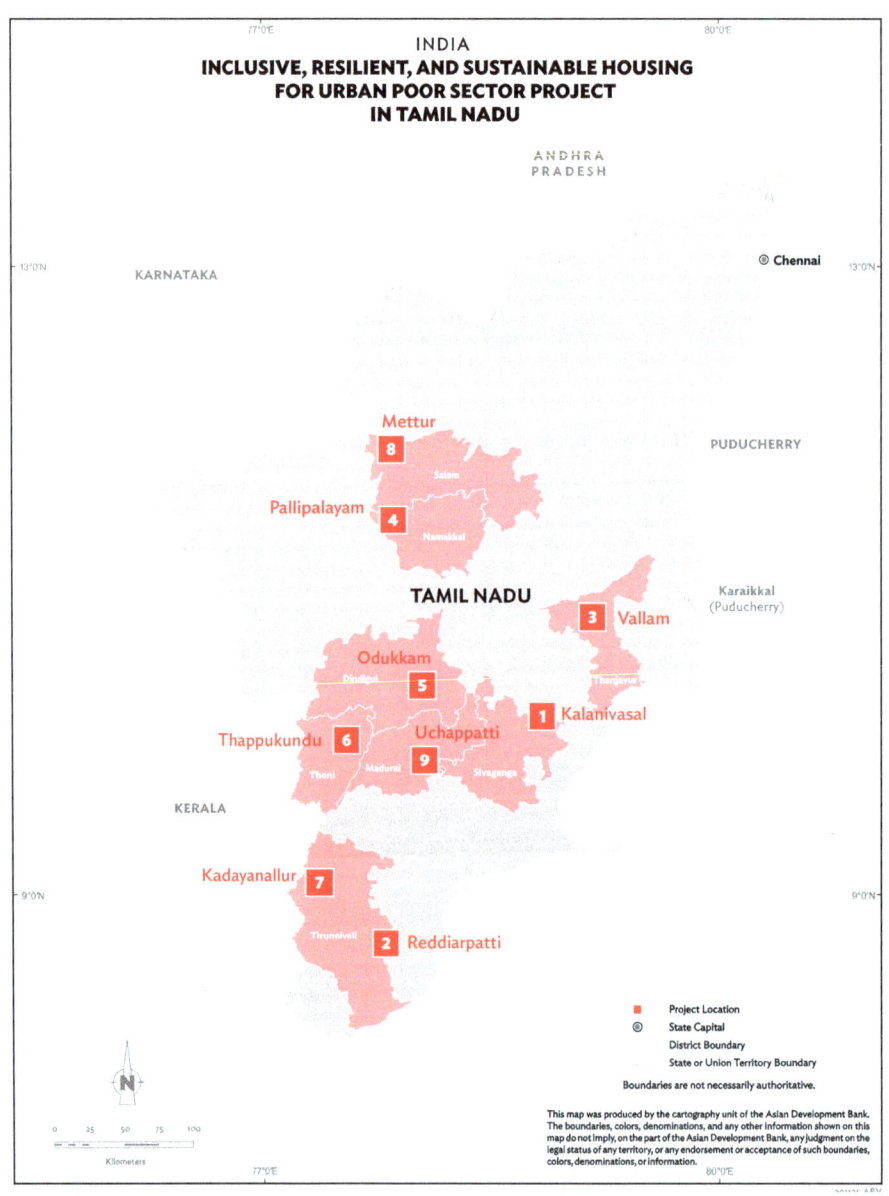

Figure 9: The Scale of Tamil Nadu's Housing Shortage

Urbanization and Population

more than
72 million
population

6th most populous state in India

One of the most highest rates of urbanization in India

48% of the population living in urban areas

Slum Population

5.8 million slum residents in Tamil Nadu

16.5% of the state's urban population

17% of the national urban population

8.9% of the national slum population

6.5% of the state's urban population live below the state poverty line of INR 937 per capita per month

among the five states that account for 62% of the country's slum population

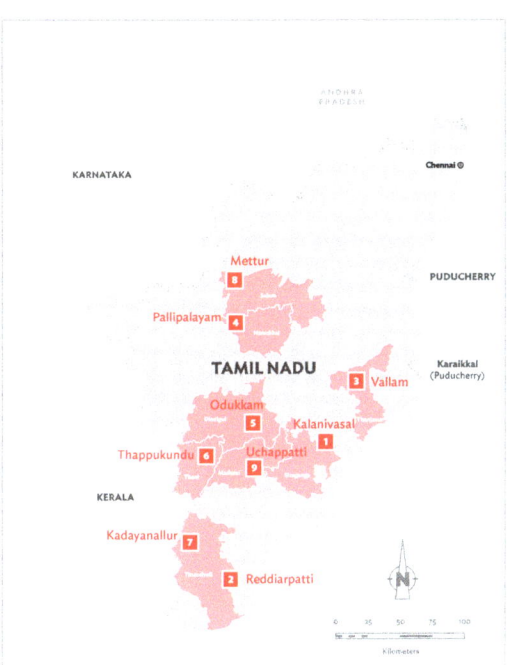

Economic Contribution

8% contribution to India's gross domestic product

Share of Housing Shortage

4% Middle Income Group or higher

Housing Demand

1.40 million units
total demand for affordable housing

0.63 million units
approved to date

40% Lowest Income Groups; INR 600,000 ($8,100)

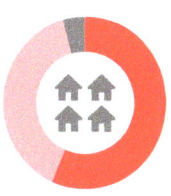
56% Economically weaker sections; annual household incomes INR 300,000 ($4,050)

Sources: (i) Government of India, Planning Commission. 2014. (ii) Data-book Compiled for Use of Planning Commission. Delhi. Government of India, Planning Commission. (iii) Report of the Expert Group to Review the Methodology for Measurement of Poverty. June 2014. http://planningcommission.nic.in/reports/genrep/pov_rep0707.pdf. Government of India, Ministry of Housing and Urban Poverty Alleviation (MHUPA), National Buildings Organisation (NBO). 2015. (iv) Slums in India: A Statistical Compendium 2015. Delhi.

Tamil Nadu is experiencing some of India's most rapid urbanization and this is bearing down hardest on the state's housing sector on a scale beyond its capacity to address alone. Tamil Nadu is the country's sixth most populous state with 72 million people and has one of the highest urbanization rates with 48% of the state's population living in cities. Nearly 17% of the state's urban population live in slums because of a lack of affordable housing for low-income families and migrant workers. The state government estimates 1.4 million housing units are needed. As of 2021, it had approved only 760,000 (54%). Middle- and upper-income households account for only 4% of the state's housing shortage.

Over 95% of the required housing stock is for the urban poor. This economically weaker section accounts for 56% of the housing shortage while the lowest income group accounts for 39%.[4]

In the absence of government and market solutions, the urban poor have resolved their housing issues as best they can by settling on land close to their jobs, which typically provide only a daily subsistence income. These 'lands of last resort' are unoccupied for a reason. They are vulnerable to hazards such as flooding from nearby waterways and soil erosion that can lead to landslides and land subsidence that can lead to more flooding. Their communities are a scene not unusual to many parts of Asia and the Pacific. What sets Tamil Nadu apart is the scale of the problem.

The government is unable to meet the housing demand without two kinds of external support: financing from the private sector and technical assistance to improve outcomes. Where the state has constructed affordable housing projects, the occupancy rates are stubbornly low at 40%. Most locations are an impractical distance from urban centers where job opportunities are. Other factors, such as the unit designs that affect community cohesiveness and functionality, proved untenable for the intended occupants. Most people have either refused to move or returned to their original homes or other informal settlements.

Ultimately, the state government and the urban poor are operating from different risk management strategies. The state government is managing risks associated with hazardous land sites and inadequate shelter, while low-income households are managing the risks of not earning enough to provide for their daily family needs. The state government and the urban poor need housing solutions that address both kinds of risks.

Project-based Solutions

To make affordable housing projects more attractive to the private sector and low-income households, government approaches need to evolve through capacity building to consider the needs of the poor by consulting them and choosing sites that align with regional development plans for long-term growth.

Innovations and Firsts

- Integrated approach to affordable housing and economic resilience, ecological urban restoration, and regional planning.
- Incorporate private operations and maintenance contracts (O&M) to protect housing assets.
- Uses a 'graduation program' to provide beneficiaries with coaching through the resettlement transition to increase their chances of thriving socially and economically in their new residential communities.

---

4   The Government of India defines economicially weaker sections and lower income groups as households with annual household incomes of INR 300,000 ($4,050), and INR 600,000 ($8,100) respectively.

Advocating for Innovations

Rarely is relocation the primary development objective of an ADB-supported project. Resettlement is often the consequence of a different development objective. For example, land is required for building or creating a non-housing related public asset, such as a wastewater treatment plant or a hydropower reservoir. Government sponsored resettlement may reflect a higher-priority development plan for land where the poor are settled. In this project, the government wanted a resettlement project that would address environmental threats to informal housing sites. The state's poorest and most vulnerable residents often live on hazard-prone land because of a lack of alternative housing options. However, government sponsored resettlement efforts are often beset with challenges that result in low occupancy of public housing.

ADB's project design team identified three opportunities for improving public housing programs in Tamil Nadu. First, they chose relocation sites close to job and income opportunities in both formal and informal sectors. Second, they consulted with the intended beneficiaries to identify risks and potential risk mitigations, such as supplementary livelihood programs and socially appropriate and preferred residential designs and amenities. Third, development and economic planning needs to integrate regional and affordable housing development aligns geographically with and growth.

Who to help first? With nearly six million slum residents across Tamil Nadu and 1.4 million housing units needed, where to begin? The project design team decided, with the government, to prioritize residents of informal settlements on hazard-prone land, such as those near dangerous waterways and erosion-prone land. It was not possible to keep those settlements where they were, as these locations will be repeatedly affected by hazard events. This decision led to the identification of nine priority sites across the central and southwest part of the state. The project will create 6,000 new affordable housing units.

Where to develop the best affordable housing? "Our number one criteria was to rule out sites that would bring unnecessary hardship to those relocating. Relocating is hard enough, let's not make it harder," said Ricardo Carlos Barba, Principal Safeguards Specialist and Team Leader for the project. "Sites should be 30 minutes travel time or less to jobs is an example of the criteria we used to select housing sites."

During project processing, Barba and his team worked with the government to develop site selection criteria based on environmental and social safeguards. The objective of the criteria was to promote and ensure high occupancy levels. The criteria ruled out, for example, sites that would have transferred households from one hazard-prone site to another. The subproject selection criteria also addressed proximity of a site to services, identifying any gaps that the project would need to fill at the potential site. Employment potential around the sites was also studied. The project could not ensure job continuity for all relocated persons, but extensive data was collected to develop strategies for relocated households.

Although the government had agreed to the criteria, they still proposed sites that did not meet all the agreed criteria. After a few iterations of proposing unsuitable sites only to have them rejected, Barba said the government quickly improved their process of assessing sites. By remaining engaged and experiencing the success of selecting sites that meet the more stringent pro-poor criteria, ADB believes the government is more likely to apply the same standard and criteria in selecting future relocation sites, whether or not ADB is involved.

The design process. The design team ensured that consultation and participation processes functioned as key elements of the government's design process. Changes must be gradually introduced. For example, in the first phase of the project, some aspects of public housing designs cannot be negotiated, such as unit sizes, regardless

Uniquely Urban—Case Studies in Innovative Urban Development

Beyond slum upgrades. ADB's support for affordable housing for low-income residents in Tamil Nadu prioritizes proximity to job centers in cities, unit designs that build community cohesiveness and functionality, and a programmatic graduation approach to support high occupancy rates among new residents.

of the number of occupants. Such a design change requires policy change. Other design alterations were more feasible, such as universal access, optimal light and airflow, enhanced safety, and accommodations for livestock.

Barba recalls early discussions with women in existing relocation sites. They said, "we are the ones who spend most of the time in these units, yet the housing complex doesn't fit our needs, such as the location of the kitchen and our preference for communal laundry washing." Consultations also brought out anxieties residents had experienced with some modern amenities such as elevators. "Going through consultations on the proposed units with future residents, one question that reoccurred was about elevators; they were worried about elevators," Barba said. With this kind of feedback, the project designers could address these problematic features or at least inform the project team of what to focus on in transition programs and raise the awareness of residents to new living arrangements.

 Thriving—It's about thriving! This is so much more than a resettlement or housing project. It really is a poverty reduction project.

— Ricardo Carlos Barba, principal safeguards specialist

To what extent. Early in the design process, the design team began deliberating over how to leverage housing for other development outcomes, especially the economic stability of project beneficiaries. "We needed a more integrated approach; not just moving slum households," Barba said. The project team collaborated with

Uniquely Urban—Case Studies in Innovative Urban Development

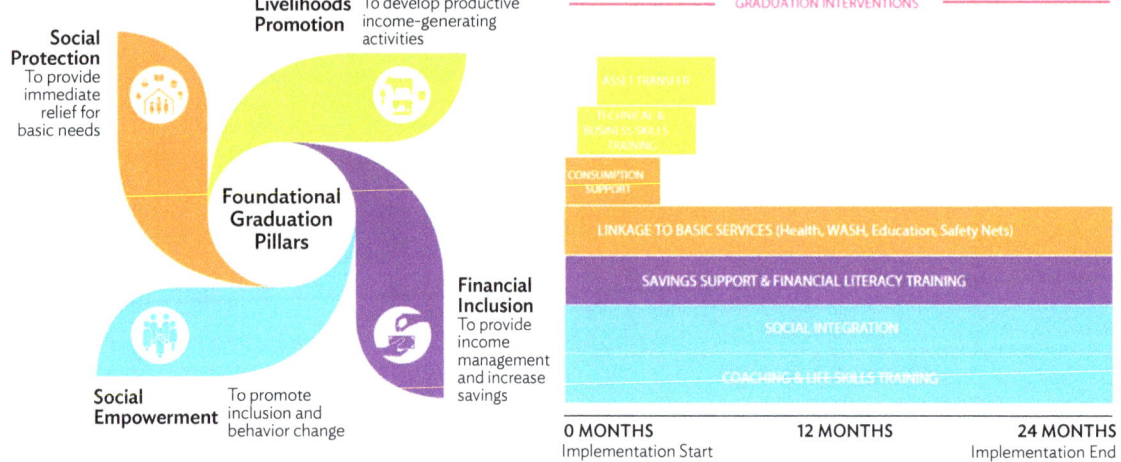

What is the Graduation Approach?

A combination of comprehensive, multi-dimensional and sequenced supports that create a 'big push' to propel the extreme poor from poverty. Often referred to as Graduation, cash plus, productive inclusion, economic inclusion, and other names.

What does it mean to graduate?

To be considered 'graduated,' households meet specific social and economic thresholds referred to as graduation criteria that address the multidimensional barriers they face.

Partnering for the poor. ADB is partnering with BRAC, a highly effective nongovernment organization specializing in poverty reduction, to implement its 'graduation program' for especially vulnerable project beneficiaries. The 18 to 36 month small group coaching program promotes livelihoods, ensures social protection and financial inclusion, and develops a sense of social empowerment. Ultimately, the graduation program hopes to retain residents in the new communities.

BRAC, a highly effective Bangladesh nongovernment organization specializing in poverty reduction, to develop a 'graduation program' for especially vulnerable households. BRAC's pioneering graduation approach is an 18 to 36 month small group coaching program that promotes livelihoods, ensures social protection and financial inclusion, and develops a sense of social empowerment. "Thriving—It's about thriving!" Barba said. "This project is so much more than building houses and resettling people. It really is a poverty reduction project."

Project Basics

The project used the sector loan modality to enable the redesign of successive subprojects when lessons, successful practices, and incremental approaches need to be adopted from previous subprojects. The risk profile of economically weak households has unique characteristics that must allow for design variations in the sequencing of changes they will experience in relocating. The sector loan modality was also the right choice because the state government already had a sector development plan in place and the institutional capacity to implement it, though it needed further support. Housing policies were also in place and the World Bank is supporting further reforms.

The project is organized into two outputs to contribute to the state's housing shortage, (i) address the unique housing needs of women and migrant urban workers, and (ii) support regional planning. See Box 6 for a summary of intended results.

From At-Risk Housing to Well-Maintained, Sustainable Communities
Besides resettling 6,000 households to safe affordable housing, the project is introducing changes to the state government's approach to affordable housing development. Specifically, the project is introducing robust operation and management schemes to encourage a higher occupancy rate and to prevent housing from slipping into slum-like conditions due to neglect. Consultations with beneficiaries and their participation is also being demonstrated as standard good practice. Working closely with beneficiaries is taken a step further with a graduation program for exceptionally vulnerable households.

"Once the land has been cleared, we have to close the loop," Barba said. "Residents should not return to the cleared land. The project will be piloting ways to secure the land to prevent further re-encroachment and restoring these areas to their full ecological function. For example, encroached waterways that have become clogged will be cleared to restore their natural flood prevention functions."

Demonstrating Public-Private Partnerships for Industrial Housing
To generate more private sector interest in affordable housing, the project is providing $35 million in equity to the Tamil Nadu Shelter Fund (TNSF). The project is piloting how a public-private partnership structure can successfully contribute to further closing the housing gap. The shelter fund is a versatile vehicle to attract private investments to deliver affordable housing, including for working women and industrial workers. The fund may establish specific special purpose vehicles to directly fund affordable housing projects or to invest in private-led affordable housing projects.

Connecting Housing to Regional Planning
Another ADB value addition supports regional planning. The state needs more geographically balanced growth but also growth that considers housing along with economic development. ADB will help develop regional plans to ensure they include affordable housing, infrastructure development, environmental protection, disaster risk management, and gender-responsiveness.

> **BOX 6**
>
> ## Summary of Intended Results
>
> **OUTCOME**
>
> **Vulnerable and disadvantaged communities in Tamil Nadu gain better access to inclusive and safe affordable housing and services. By 2029:**
> - 5% increase in affordable housing for economically weaker sections and low-income groups in project districts.
> - At least 60% housing occupancy rate for project-built affordable housing for economically weaker sections and low-income groups in project districts.
> - Total occupancy of project-built or renovated industrial housing and women's hostels for low-income migrant workers increased by at least 4,400, of which women occupy 400.
>
> **OUTPUT 1**
>
> **Affordable and improved housing for vulnerable communities constructed. By 2028:**
> - At least 6,000 affordable housing units constructed in nine projects sites with climate- and disaster-resilient and gender-responsive features and provisions for basic urban services and amenities.
> - 60% of relocated vulnerable households, including 50% women registrants and all transgender beneficiaries registered in the graduation program in pilot locations.
> - Improved operation and maintenance schemes for safe gender-responsive shelter piloted in five housing sites.
> - Waterways cleared, protected, and ecologically restored in two sites.
>
> To be funded by the technical assistance grant and completed by 2025:
>
> - Housing delivery methodologies and systems for the urban poor, including operation and management modalities, asset management, beneficiary survey and data management, and ecological restoration alternatives developed.
> - At least 100 eligible staff from the Housing and Urban Development Department, Tamil Nadu Slum Clearance Board, and urban local bodies (including at least 80% of eligible women staff) report awareness on good practices and lessons on urban poor housing operations and maintenance (O&M) modalities, asset management, beneficiary data management, and ecological restoration.
>
> **OUTPUT 2**
>
> **More affordable housing for urban poor and migrant workers. By 2028:**
> - Total fund size of Tamil Nadu Shelter Fund increased to at least $200 million. 2020 baseline: $57 million.
> - Total capacity for women's hostel beds for low-income women migrant workers increased by 500.
> - Total capacity for industrial housing beds for low-income migrant workers increased by 5,000.

To be funded by the technical assistance grant and completed by 2025:

- O&M modalities and model contracts developed.
- Pipeline developed for affordable housing projects with private sector involvement for migrant economically weaker sections, lower-income groups, and other vulnerable groups.
- At least 50 eligible staff report awareness on good practices and lessons on (i) O&M modalities, (ii) private sector engagement, and (iii) delivery of affordable housing for migrant economically weaker sections, lower-income groups, and other vulnerable groups. Eligible staff are from Tamil Nadu Infrastructure Fund Management Corporation, investee special purpose vehicle staff, and O&M staff of private sector projects, including at least 80% of eligible women staff.

Regional plan development supported. By 2028:

- Integrated regional plan formulated and submitted to government for Tamil Nadu's industrial corridor (i.e. Chennai-Kanyakumari Industrial Corridor) that includes affordable housing, environmental management and disaster resilience, and gender mainstreaming formulated and submitted to the government for approval.
- Subsequent integrated regional plans for 30 districts following the model in contracts completed.

Note: Unless otherwise stated, the baseline is zero or not applicable.
Source: ADB. 2021. *Report and Recommendations to the President: Proposed Loans and Technical Assistance Grant for the Inclusive, Resilient and Sustainable Housing for Urban Poor Sector Project in Tamil Nadu, India*. Manila.

Concerns for Sustainability and Impact

The project design addresses common risks in resettlement processes for people and assets, as well as long-term growth and financing in the sector to prevent the expansion and intensification of slums. "There may be criticism of the project that relocation is a poor option in dealing with slums. But with people living in hazard-prone areas, practically living in waterways, they can't stay in these areas. It's not safe," Barba said. "Given the need to relocate, we need to see models that work with the most vulnerable."

Social sustainability. Families not building resilience to the changes that are part of resettling is a risk to the social impacts the project aspires to achieve. Therefore, as part of the implementation, the project pilots a program with BRAC that will be replicated by government at all the housing sites. Attention is paid to customized household support to improve their chances of thriving socially and economically in their newly resettled housing. With the project team, World Vision India worked with potential beneficiaries. The graduation program organizes households according to their vulnerability levels, assesses local markets for income opportunities, connects households with trained program field staff for coaching support, and conducts training on livelihood development. The interventions are based on household needs and the local context. Through the process, the implementing agencies learn ways of making future relocations more successful for households.

Asset sustainability. Effective operations and maintenance (O&M) of the new housing is important for long-term sustainability. The project will provide initial financing for O&M through the implementation period until 2028, which will be contracted to the private sector from the time of commissioning. After the first three years of the implementation period, the Tamil Nadu Urban Habitat Development Board (TNUHDB) is expected to have a time-bound action plan for the efficient turnover of O&M responsibilities. The first five years after construction, the project will finance contracts between TNUHDB and a private O&M provider. To ensure long-term sustainability and financial viability, TNUHDB will shift maintenance costs from the municipality to residents through incremental increases in maintenance charges. The technical assistance grant accompanying the loan includes support for preparing the O&M contracts and O&M models for the different housing subprojects. The O&M studies will inform the structure of maintenance charges and provide other useful financial information. The technical assistance is also supporting the development of an electronic asset registry for TNUHDB.

Sustainable financing. ADB's equity in Class B shares of the project's special project vehicles are expected to attract direct private sector investment. In addition, ADB's funds will promote sustainable affordable housing development through private O&M operators. The project is also an opportunity to demonstrate to the private sector the capacity of the Tamil Nadu government and housing agencies.

Learn More

➦ Read project documents from adb.org: https://www.adb.org/projects/53067-004/main

Contact:	**Ricardo Carlos Barba,** rbarba@adb.org
	Sourav Majumder, smajumder@adb.org

INDIA, INDONESIA, PHILIPPINES, THAILAND

Indorama Ventures Regional Blue Loan Project

ADB's First Blue Loan Intercepts Plastics from Landfills, Oceans through Recycling, and Reuse of Ubiquitous PET

with Shuji Hashizume, Daniel Wiedmer, Deborah Robertson, and James G. Baker

Project Name	Indorama Ventures Regional Blue Loan Project
Project Location	India, Indonesia, Philippines, Thailand
ADB Department	Private Sector Operations Department
Division	Infrastructure Finance Division 2
Sector	Urban solid waste management
Loan Approval Date	October 2020
Loan	$100 million
Total Project Cost	$300 million
Borrower	Indorama Ventures Global Services Limited
Financial Modalities	Nonsovereign LIBOR Based Loan (Regular Loan): Ordinary Capital Resources
Co-Financing	Leading Asia's Private Infrastructure Fund (LEAP) Co-financing of $50 million
	Modality and Sources ($50 million)
	Others ($200 million)
Project Scope	Provide financing for the expansion of regional recycling operations to reduce plastic waste in landfills and oceans.
Design Team Leader(s)	Shuji Hashizume, Principal Investment Specialist, Infrastructure Finance Division 2, Private Sector Operations Department
Project Advisor	Daniel Wiedmer, Principal Investment Specialist, Infrastructure Finance Division 2, Private Sector Operations Department

Source: ADB. 2020. Report and Recommendation to the President: Indorama Ventures Regional Blue Loan Project. Manila.

The Development Needs

Marine pollution from plastic waste is a complex multisectoral challenge. The world needs solutions that:

- Reduce plastic waste and its environmental impacts.
- Divert plastic waste away from landfills and oceans.
- Redesign, recover, and reuse plastic products and materials.
- Improve collection and recycle systems.
- Increase the circularity of plastic packaging.

We need the private sector to contribute solutions to the plastics problem through their supply chains or intervene in the lifecycle of plastics. For example, global food and beverage companies are increasingly using recycled materials for their products.

Specifically, polyethylene terephthalate (PET) plastic, widely used in beverage bottles, needs better collection, sorting, and recycling to reduce plastic waste in landfills and oceans.

Development Challenges

- Solid waste management and recycling systems have not effectively captured massive volumes of single-use, non-degradable plastic packaging, the most common item found during international coastal cleanups. Landfills and oceans are overwhelmed with low-value, single-use, non-degradable plastic.

Plastic is a preferred material for consumer packaging because it is cheap, available, and versatile. As of 2015, half of the world's plastics were produced in Asia and the plastics industry contributes to poverty reduction and income generation in emerging markets. Plastic performs well—until it becomes waste.

The virtues of plastic are also what has made it such an environmental villain. It has a low residual value, is often used only once before it is discarded, and is non-degradable. As a result, it makes up a large volume of the waste in landfills and oceans.

Plastics production has soared from 15 million tons in 1964 to 211 million tons in 2014,[5] becoming a primary culprit of natural resource depletion, waste, environmental degradation, and climate change, along with adverse health effects (Figure 10).

---

5   Ocean Conservancy and McKinsey Center for Business and Environment. 2015. Stemming the Tide: Land-based Ocean Strategies for a Plastics Free Ocean. Washington, D.C. as quoted in ADB. 2020. Report and Recommendation to the President: Indorama Ventures Regional Blue Loan Project. Manila.

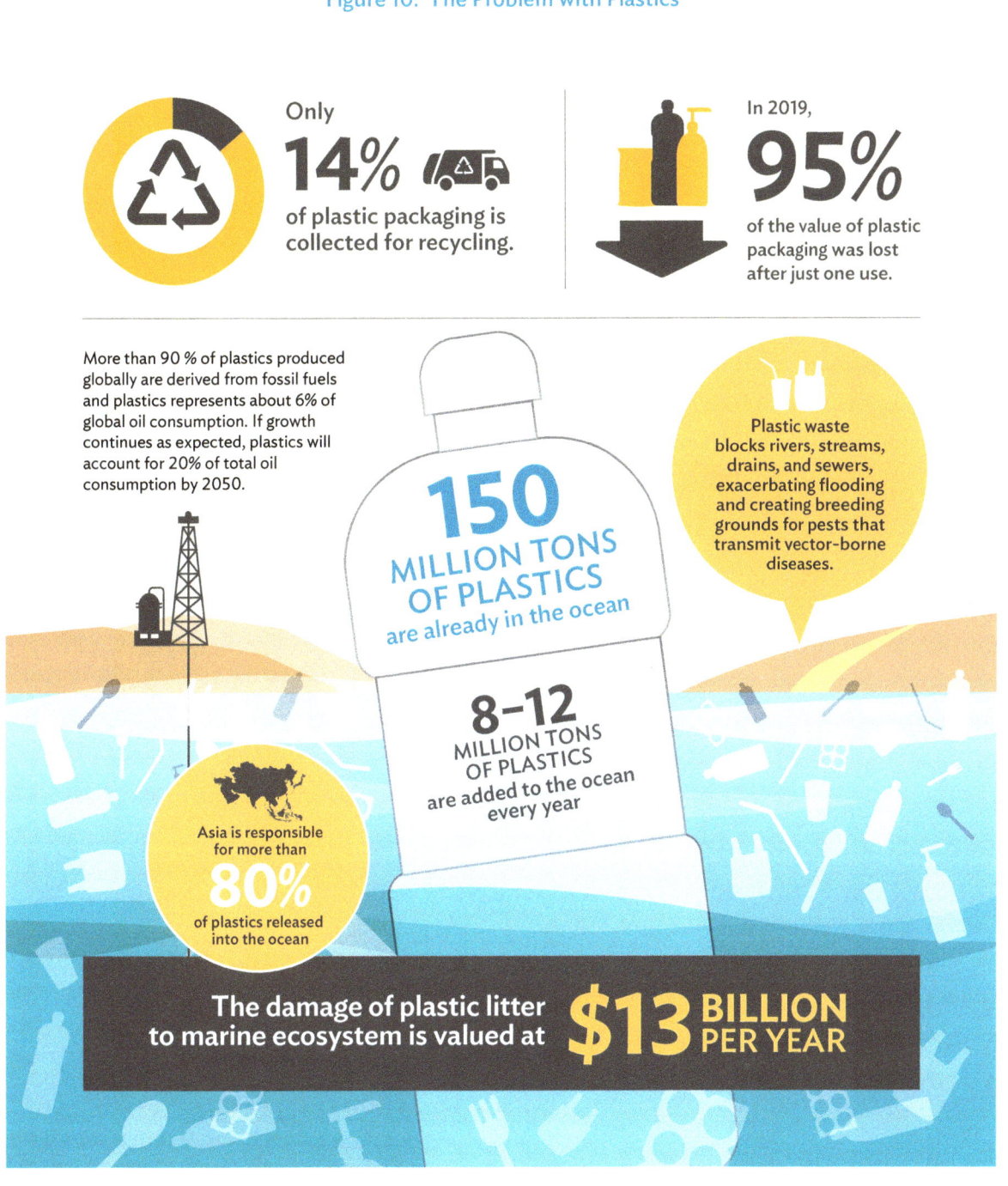

Figure 10: The Problem with Plastics

a World Economic Forum, Ellen MacArthur Foundation and McKinsey & Company. 2016. The New Plastics Economy: Rethinking the Future of Plastics. Cowes, United Kingdom.
b United Nations Environment Programme. 2014. Valuing Plastics: The Business Case for Measuring, Managing and Disclosing Plastic Use in the Consumer Goods Industry. Nairobi.

Source: All as quoted in ADB. 2020. Report and Recommendation to the President: Indorama Ventures Regional Blue Loan Project. Manila.

Single-use plastics. Emerging markets need better value chains for processing the ubiquitous single-use plastic container and packaging, effectively intercepting them from polluting oceans and taking up precious landfill space (photo: Indorama Ventures Public Company Limited).

Project-based Solutions

Support the reduction of plastic waste and pollution by supporting global producers of recycled polyethylene terephthalate (rPET) in their efforts to increase their operational capacity to aggregate post-consumer PET, produce higher volumes of rPET, and supply it as packaging and other materials.

Innovations and Firsts

- ADB's first nonsovereign blue loan, internationally verified, will expand plastic recycling operations to avert plastic waste in landfills and oceans.

ADB's private sector and sovereign operations staff collaborated to enter the plastics market in a substantial way. "There are issues on both the government and private sector sides," Wiedmer said. "We can work together from both sides."

A Development Opportunity in PET, rPET

To contribute to reducing plastic waste and promoting a circular economy with plastics, the ADB project team looked to PET, a common material for beverage bottles. Of all the plastics, PET is one of the more environmentally friendly. It has all the qualities that make it possible to recycle it repeatedly (durable, transparent, lightweight, non-reactive, cost effective, and thermally stable). In 2018, global demand for PET reached 25.8 million tons annually.

PET has a recycling rate higher than other plastics. However, about half the PET produced is not collected for recycling, and only 7% is recycled bottle-to-bottle—representing a significant environmental loss. For PET to achieve its recycling potential, the value chain needs better collection and sorting systems to produce more rPET into PET products. Sorting is key to salvaging plastics from incineration, which results in greenhouse gas emissions.

Recycled PET (rPET) is more expensive to produce than pure PET. Still, global food and beverage companies are under increasing regulatory pressure to use more recycled plastics in their packaging, especially in the European Union. The regulations are working. The Coca-Cola Company was planning to use 100% rPET for bottle production in Sweden (in 2020) and the Netherlands and Norway (in 2021), the first countries in its global production network to do so.[6]

"I think we are seeing a transition to recycling and efficiency," Wiedmer said. "Demand for rPET will dramatically increase."

ADB Provides Recycling Support to World's Largest PET Producer

To address marine plastic pollution, ADB identified Indorama Ventures Global Services Limited (IVL) as a reputable partner. A Thailand-based global petrochemical producer, IVL is the world's largest integrated PET producer, operating 110 manufacturing facilities in 22 countries across five continents. It can produce an rPET for bottle-to-bottle recycling.

> IVL's PET recycling is really well established in developed markets but the challenge is in emerging markets, like Southeast Asia. Indorama needed financing and it wanted the blue loan certification."

— Daniel Wiedmer, Principal Investment Specialist

IVL has well-established, long-term sales relationships with global beverage companies. "It is one of the largest but has also faced growing pressure to commit to the climate change agenda and to reducing greenhouse gas emissions," Wiedmer said. IVL has pledged to recycle 750,000 tons of post-consumer PET bottles by 2025 to fulfill its obligation as a signatory to the New Plastics Economy Global Commitment.[7] To do this, IVL needed to strengthen its collection and sorting systems that provide the material for its rPET manufacturing.

"IVL's PET recycling is really well established in developed markets but the challenge is in emerging markets, like Southeast Asia," Wiedmer said. "Indorama needed financing and it wanted the blue loan certification."

---

6   For more information on how one bottling company is shifting toward 100% recycled PET (rPET) see https://www.coca-colacompany.com/news/packaging-sustainability-in-united-states.
7   As explained in ADB. 2020. Report and Recommendation to the President: Indorama Ventures Regional Blue Loan Project. Manila: Ellen MacArthur Foundation. New Plastics Economy. Launched in 2018 by the United Nations Environment Programme and the Ellen McArthur Foundation, the New Plastics Economy aims to create long-term systemic value by fostering a working after-use economy, drastically reducing leakage and decoupling plastics from fossil feedstocks. More than 400 organizations have joined the movement and many top tier companies such as The Coca-Cola Company, Nestlé, S.A. , and Unilever Plc. have pledged to make their packaging reusable, recyclable or compostable.

ADB's Private Sector Operations Department (PSOD) had processed loans for renewable energy and green bonds, including the first green loan in Southeast Asia, but it had not yet processed a blue loan. ADB partnered with the World Bank's International Finance Corporation (IFC), which offered a larger team of experts. IFC co-financed $150 million of the total $300 million project cost, all debt financed.

Sorting plastic reusables. Workers in Indorama's Thailand polyethylene terephthalate (PET) facility sort single-use plastic bottles for manufacturing recycled PET (rPET) or recycled PET for bottle-to-bottle recycling (photo: Indorama Ventures Public Company Limited).

A Global and ADB First

This is ADB's first blue loan under its Ocean Finance Framework.[8] The loan also follows the Blue Bond Guidelines of the Blue Natural Capital Financing Facility, as verified by DNV GL. The loan is also the world's first blue loan to a global plastics resin manufacturer.[9] The blue loan was part of ADB's pioneering Blue Bond, issued in September 2021.[10]

ADB's environmental and social safeguards policies and teams were an incentive for Indorama to seek multilateral finance, which offered integrity to their efforts to recycle and transfer social and environmental knowledge to improve overall corporate practices.

---

8   ADB. 2020. Ocean Finance Framework. Manila.
9   World Bank. 2020. New Blue Loan to Help Indorama Ventures Recycle 50 Billion polyethylene terephthalate (PET) Bottles a Year by 2025. https://pressroom.ifc.org/all/pages/PressDetail.aspx?ID=26079
10 ADB. ADB Blue Bonds. 2021. https://www.adb.org/sites/default/files/publication/731026/adb-sovereign-blue-bonds-start-guide.pdf

"This was a little outside our normal domain of energy, transport, or urban development," Wiedmer said. "The challenge was whether this was something we could get comfortable with, which is what the risk analysis and sector analysis is for."

Project Basics

ADB's financing is a general corporate loan. IVL on-lends to its operations in India, Indonesia, the Philippines, and Thailand to build new plants that will recycle PET into rPET materials for bottles and other PET end-uses. The new plants are expected to be fully operational by 2022 and will divert nearly five billion additional bottles from the environment. The investment will also support IVL's move toward more environmentally sustainable operations, including energy efficiency measures and the use of clean energy. IVL will also transfer advanced technologies from its rPET facilities in Europe and the United States to ADB's developing member countries.

The loan contributes to ADB's Action Plan for Healthy Oceans and Sustainable Blue Economies, which aims to increase investments and technical assistance to $5 billion during 2019–2024.

Blue Loan. ADB's first nonsovereign Blue Loan is enabling Indorama Ventures Public Company Limited (IVL) to expand its recycling operations in India, Indonesia, the Philippines, and Thailand. The new plants, expected to be fully operational in 2022, will divert nearly five billion additional bottles from the environment. (Photo: Indorama Ventures Public Company Limited).

Concerns for Sustainability and Impact

One of the main risks and challenges to Indorama's plans to recycle 750,000 tons of post-consumer PET bottles by 2025 and expand its operations in Southeast Asia is its ability to work out the collection and sorting systems to supply its new plants with the PET materials to recycle. The collections systems are not yet officially established but are part of the work in constructing the new plants. "The collection systems differ between countries," Wiedmer explained. "Many systems are informal, and Indorama will collaborate with aggregators for a stable supply. For example, in the Philippines, Indorama is partnering with The Coca-Cola Company to leverage its distribution systems for collection, providing shops and sellers with PET bottle collection receptacles."

Notes on Replication

The Indorama project is a case study in working with big corporations interested in taking bigger steps forward. Wiedmer recalls both enthusiastic support for the project as it was being designed but also skepticism as to why ADB would assist an already well-capitalized, global corporation and why PET, which is the easiest plastic to recycle and collect.

"I can understand why it was confusing," Wiedmer said. "Indorama is a big company, and they are sophisticated in their business, but recycling is a new area for them, and they had not yet expanded PET recycling to emerging markets in a meaningful way. They have experience but recycling in developing countries is not comparable to their business-as-usual lines."

Supporting Indorama became an opportunity to affect industry standards for collection, sorting, and recycling in environmentally and socially sustainable ways with ADB's involvement. Other companies are now expressing an interest in ADB financing.

Learn More

- Watch a video on ADB's Action Plan for Healthy Oceans and Sustainable Blue Economies: https://vimeo.com/332898098
- About this project: https://www.adb.org/projects/54333-001/main
- About ADB's Action Plan for Healthy Oceans and Sustainable Blue Economies: https://www.adb.org/news/adb-launches-5-billion-healthy-oceans-action-plan
- About ADB's Oceans Financing Initiative: https://www.adb.org/sites/default/files/related/145041/Oceans%20Financing%20Initiative.pdf
- About ADB's Blue Bonds https://www.adb.org/news/adb-issues-first-blue-bond-ocean-investments. https://www.adb.org/sites/default/files/publication/756966/adb-blue-bonds.pdf

Contact:	Daniel Wiedmer, dwiedmer@adb.org
	Shuji Hashizume, shashizume@adb.org

GEORGIA

Georgia Green Bond Project

7

Private Sector Team in Georgia Expands Green Bond Market in Asia, Urban Water Sector

with David Urbaneja-Furelos

Project Name	Georgia Green Bond Project
Project Location	Georgia, with specific investments in Tbilisi Urban Region
ADB Team	Private Sector Operations Department/Infrastructure Finance Division 1
Sector	Urban water supply
Year Approved	2020
Borrower	Georgia Global Utilities JSC
Loan Amount	$20 million
Financial Modalities	Nonsovereign Debt Security (Regular Loan): Ordinary capital resources
Other financing	$20 million in modality and sources $20 million in co-financing from Leading Asia's Private Infrastructure Fund (LEAP) $210 million, other project costs not financed by ADB or co-financing
Project Scope	Support a green bond issuance in Georgia for the rehabilitation and expansion of Tbilisi's water infrastructure and demonstrate green bond investor interest
Design Team Leader(s)	David Urbaneja-Furelos, Investment Specialist, Infrastructure Finance Division 1, Private Sector Operations Department (Georgia Resident Mission)

The Development Need

Despite the uncertainty that spread across global markets from the Coronovirus disease (COVID-19) pandemic, private utility companies continued to feel the pressure to stay the course on critical capital investments in systems and maintain momentum on their climate commitments, even though that momentum was at a slower pace. COVID-19 stay-at-home and shelter-in-place public orders and economic shutdowns caused wild shifts in demand for and scrutiny of water supply, wastewater, and energy systems. The clear skies the world temporarily enjoyed without planes, trains, and automobiles signaled the elasticity of what is economically, environmentally, and socially possible.

Before COVID-19, investors and producers worldwide were attuning their portfolios and operations to depend less on fossil fuels and retrofit for more automated, digital, secure smart systems to produce cleaner, more efficient products and services. COVID-19's uncertainty and adverse economic effects tightened the liquidity of the capital market, forcing companies to adapt their preferences and approaches to financing and operations.

Georgia Global Utilities JSC (GGU) was one such company needing capital during the pandemic. A holding company, GGU operates two primary business lines, water and renewable energy. Its water business, Georgian Water & Power (GWP), is the largest privately-owned utility in Georgia, serving 35% of the population. GGU's energy business line operates eight hydropower plants and one wind power plant, providing Georgia with more than 7.5% of its installed power capacity. GGU, in turn, is a wholly owned subsidiary of JSC Georgia Capital, which is 100% owned by Georgia Capital PLC, a London Stock Exchange-listed entity. Georgia Capital PLC is one of Georgia's most reputable and profitable business groups. Between GWP and GGU's other water subsidiaries, they are the sole supplier of Tbilisi's water and sanitation services and nearby municipalities—a natural monopoly.

Before the pandemic, GGU had embarked on a capital expenditure program to rehabilitate its water supply and sanitation systems to improve water quality. Georgia's water pipelines and networks are dilapidated, with significant leakage and revenue losses after years of under-investment before the government privatized the utility in 2007. Confronted with the tightened liquidity of capital markets, GGU was searching for new sources to continue its capital investments.

Outside the developing countries, green bonds have proven to be a popular, innovative financial instrument for investments in environmental or climate-benefiting projects. They are noted for offering investors transparency and accountability. A team from ADB's PSOD believed green bonds were an answer to GGU's need.

Core Development Challenges

- Limited market for green bonds in Asia and the Pacific because of unfamiliarity and inexperience among potential issuers and investors.
- COVID-19 volatility, even in the bond market.

Project-based Solutions

ADB's experience with green bonds was both a selling point and a risk. ADB had experience structuring green bonds, but its experience was limited to Southeast Asia, mainly the Philippines and Thailand. Like much of the developing countries, the rest of Asia and the Pacific had yet to wade into green bonds.

"Bonds are the best way to co-finance. It's a way to test the market's confidence in a company. Will investors buy?" said David Urbaneja-Furelos, an investment specialist with ADB's PSOD. Green bond projects can afford lighter covenants because the market decides what is attractive and safe enough for investing. International finance institutions (IFI) offer due diligence on the bond and issuer, which was just as accurate before COVID-19. However, the pandemic brought a new wariness to bonds. "With COVID-19, companies were not willing to take a risk with bonds without IFIs," Urbaneja-Furelos explained. "COVID-19 was just too new. The volatility was too high."

Innovations and First

- Establish local private sector green markets in the region.
- Demonstrate the process and viability of green bonds through a credible issuer.
- Demonstrate this in Georgia, which would be a first for the country and the South Caucasus region.

> Not every company is ready for bonds, let alone green bonds. It requires a certain sophistication and willingness to do the work."
>
> — David Urbaneja-Furelos, investment specialist, PSOD

To develop demand for green bonds among potential issuers and investors, the PSOD team determined that it needed to demonstrate the process and viability of green bonds through a successful bond issuance and subscription. To do this, the PSOD team knew from experience those credible issuers are critical to securing investor confidence. A credible issuer will abide by green bond criteria and already have demonstrated commitment to sustainability and climate resilience, adaptation, or mitigation agendas. "Not every company is ready for bonds, let alone green bonds. It requires a certain sophistication and willingness to do the work," Urbaneja-Furelos said.

ADB believed it had identified one such private issuer with GGU.

A successful green bond issuance would demonstrate the products ability to promote foreign direct investment, which will be important in post-COVID-19 recovery efforts to create more jobs and combat poverty through the growth of the private sector. For GGU, a green bond would provide capital for its rehabilitation program while also catalyzing further private sector investment in water and clean energy. A green bond issuance in Georgia could have a positive demonstration effect on the region (see Box 7 for a summary of intended results).

Advocating for Innovations

When the PSOD team approached GGU to offer financing, Urbaneja-Furelos recalled that GGU was unfamiliar with PSOD's operations and initially not interested. However, with tightening liquidity in European markets, PSOD went back to GGU to suggest a green bond issuance and emphasize ADB's value additions, such as its experience in green bonds elsewhere in Asia, the due diligence it offers investors, and incorporating other development outcomes into the project to improve the attraction and impact of the project. ADB was the first to suggest green bonds to GGU, and they had GGU's attention. "As one of the biggest companies in Georgia, they want innovation. So they were very interested in the green bond," Urbaneja-Furelos said. "They wanted to raise their profile with green bonds and be the first. They knew we would be fair and think development-minded."

As an anchor investor, ADB brought credibility to the bond and would attract local and international investors. But GGU expressed reluctance, believing ADB's processes would require more time than commercial financing from Europe. "There is outdated thinking out there among potential clients that banks in Asia cannot deliver quick enough," Urbaneja-Furelos said. "They are not entirely wrong, either. The processes here are not prepared for bonds."

ADB committed to using the Faster Approach to Small Nonsovereign Transaction (FAST) framework and guaranteed financing within 2.5 months (from initial meeting to disbursement). "This was the tightest of the tightest timelines," Urbaneja-Furelos recalled. "They also really appreciated that I was based locally and could have face-to-face meetings, even if it was only for a 15-minute discussion. It built confidence." Because of the frequent meetings, Urbaneja-Furelos said there were fewer surprises during the loan processing period, though there were still times of uncertainty. On this timeline, two weeks of uncertainty was too long.

Internally, Urbaneja-Furelos said he worked hard to promote the project during the concept and project approval stages. Internally, climate financing is a priority, yet the project did not qualify because the proceeds from ADB's bond subscription would be used to rehabilitate water assets, which do not directly reduce greenhouse gas emissions. However, 80% of ADB's funding follows the most comprehensive 2018 green bond principles.

PSOD processed the loan in eight weeks, although other IFIs are faster, such as EBRD, which supported the project but with a larger team than ADB, Urbaneja-Furelos noted. ADB was, however, the only multilateral development bank investor.

Project Basics

The project design ring-fences ADB's bond subscription for investments in the water system rehabilitation and expansion to ensure Tbilisi benefits in real development terms from the bond issuance. The improvements will plug nonrevenue water losses, salvaging at least two million cubic meters of water each year and servicing 15,000 new water connections. The project's intended outputs are summarized in Box 7. The fresh capital ensures a sustainable and affordable water supply. At the same time, other proceeds will enable GGU to consolidate and refinance debt at the holding company level while strengthening its cash balances and flexibility at the group level.

Adding value to GGU's HR Profile. Diversifying GGU's human resources in meaningful ways at policy and operational levels was an opportunity ADB recognized the project could affect, an opportunity that would have been lost had GGU pursued traditional commercial bank financing. The gender profile of GGU's employee demographics reflects national employment and gender trends, which are not all that different from elsewhere in the developing countries. Of GGU's nearly 2,500 employees, 27% work in executive, managerial, or administrative office roles, and 73% work technical jobs in the field (engineers, electricians, plumbers, etc.). Of the office staff, 45% are women, split almost evenly between middle and executive management positions. Only 18% are in top management. In addition, no women were working in the field.

To influence the corporate culture to benefit women, the project team and GGU agreed on developing a gender inclusion policy with an annual report on gender sensitivity progress within the company, an anti-sexual harassment policy with awareness-raising activities, and an internship program to create more opportunities for women interested in field positions. "Always involve gender in projects and at the highest levels." Urbaneja-Furelos said. "Be ambitious."

BOX 7

Summary of Intended Results for the Georgia Green Bond Project

OUTCOME

Ensured funding support for Georgia Global Utilities JSC's (GGU) sustainable water supply and clean power operations.[a]
- GGU green bond issuance meets interest payments and principal repayments until maturity.
- Volume of water sales increased to at least 180 million cubic meters (m^3) by 2023. 2019 baseline: 178 million cubic meters per year (m^3/year).

OUTPUT 1

Green bonds by GGU successfully issued. By 2020:
- Full subscription for $250 million green bonds issued by GGU.
- GGU, including its affiliates and subsidiaries, meet 100% of its payment obligations by 2020.

OUTPUT 2

GGU's water supply system rehabilitated and enhanced. By 2023:
- Water system capacity increased to at least 900 million m^3/year. 2019 baseline: 839 million m^3/year.
- At least 15,000 additional new connections benefiting from expanded water system. 2019 baseline: 5,439.

OUTPUT 3

GGU's capacity building opportunities for women enhanced.
- A women's networking group is established and organizes at least one online or in-person women's networking event by Q1 2021. FY2019 baseline: 0.
- At least 10 interns, 50% of whom are women, join GGU's internship program by Q3 2021. FY2019 baseline: 0, 0 women interns.

OUTPUT 4

Gender equality in GGU's staffing enhanced.
- Increase of at least 10 women staff in technical departments by 2023. 2019 baseline: 140.
- At least one gender inclusion policy on increasing women's recruitment, retention, and promotion developed, approved by management, and integrated into HR guidance documents by 2023. 2019 baseline: 0.
- At least one annual gender-sensitive report on the company's employment trends developed by Q2 2021. 2019 baseline: 0.

OUTPUT 5

Gender inclusiveness of GGU's work environment enhanced.
- A policy against sexual harassment established by Q4 2020. 2019 baseline: not applicable.
- At least one annual awareness-raising activity on the sexual harassment policy for staff conducted, potentially by a civil society organization such as a women's organization, by Q1 2021. 2019 baseline: 0.

---

[a] The Design and Monitoring Framework does not include a target date because at the outcome level they cannot be fully achieved until the end of the project. "a" is achieved immediately because it is a bond sell, but "b" does state sales should have increased by 2023.
Source: ADB. 2020. *Report and Recommendations to the President: Proposed Loans and Technical Assistance Grant.*

Concerns for Impact and Sustainability

The future is looking positive for green bonds. The Georgia Green Bond Project was over-subscribed 1.4 times. PSOD has since processed a second bond issuance, the first transport green bond with a state-owned entity. It was over-subscribed eight times. The project's approval and successful subscription "raised the standard within ADB," Urbaneja-Furelos said. "It strengthened investor confidence in a small country and during a crisis like the COVID-19 pandemic. Georgia needed this."

Learn More

Read: https://www.adb.org/projects/54300-001/main#tabs-0-2

Contact: **David Urbaneja-Furelos,**
Investment Specialist
durbanejafurelos@adb.org

MONGOLIA

Sustainable Tourism Development Project and
Sustainable Tourism Development Project (Phase 2)

Integrating Urban Design, Nature, and Heritage for Tourism in a Cold-Climate Country: Preliminary ADB Lessons from Mongolia

with Mark R. Bezuijen and Erdensaikhan Nyamjav

Project Names	Mongolia: Sustainable Tourism Development Project and Sustainable Tourism Development Project (Phase 2) (hereafter informally 'Phase 1' and 'Phase 2')
Project Location	Activities under both projects encompass urban and rural locations in five provinces in northern, northeastern, and western Mongolia, including eight protected areas.
ADB Team	East Asia Department
Sector	Industry and trade, rural sanitation, rural solid waste management, water-based natural resources management, road transport
Year Approved	Phase 1: 2019; Phase 2: 2022
Implementation Period	Phase 1: 2019–2024; Phase 2: 2022–2028
Borrower	Government of Mongolia
Financing	Phase 1: $38 million loan; Phase 2: $30.0 million loan, $2.0 million Japan Fund for Prosperous and Resilient Asia and the Pacific grant, and $650,000 High Level Technology Fund grant
Modalities	Phase 1: regular and concessional loan; Phase 2: regular loan
Scope of Projects	Support for the development of Mongolia's tourism industry, focused on nature and culture-based tourism to benefit communities, promote nature-based solutions to protect wilderness and cultural heritage, and contribute to economic recovery and resilience in the aftermath of the Coronavirus disease (COVID-19) pandemic.
Risk Categorization	Low
Design Team Leader(s)	Mark R. Bezuijen, Principal Environment Specialist, East Asia Department (EARD) Ongonsar Purev, Senior Environment Officer, EARD (Mongolia Resident Mission)
Current Project Officers	**Phase 1:** Erdenesaikhan Nyamjav, Associate Social Development Officer (Safeguards), EARD (Mongolia Resident Mission)
	Phase 2: Mark R. Bezuijen, Principal Environment Specialist, EARD
Executing Agency	Ministry of Environment and Tourism

Development Context

Before the Coronavirus disease (COVID-19) pandemic, tourism was the largest and fastest-growing sector of the global economy. About 20% of global tourism comprised ecotourism.[11] Many countries have harnessed the benefits of ecotourism for economic development, local income generation, and nature conservation based on scenic destinations, wildlife, and cultural heritage. Well-planned ecotourism leverages natural and cultural resources as assets for social and economic development.

> The government sought new tourism opportunities to help support livelihoods, the economy and protection of nature and heritage.
>
> — Ongonsar Purev, Senior Environment Officer
> for ADB's Mongolia Resident Mission, East Asia Department

Similar to global trends, tourism in Mongolia was growing rapidly prior to the COVID-19 pandemic and comprised the third-largest sector of the economy after mining and agriculture. Tourism accounted for 7% of gross domestic product (GDP), about $989 million, and was growing annually at 12%, almost double the national GDP growth rate. International arrivals in 2019 (577,300) had grown by 6% compared with 2018.[12]

Whether travelers are visiting Mongolia's capital city Ulaanbaatar or venturing out into the country's vast landscapes for a nomadic cultural experience, tourism is an opportunity for job creation and local entrepreneurship. In 2019, tourism accounted for more than 7.6% of total employment or 88,700 jobs and was projected to provide 95,000 jobs by 2030.[13]

This case study shares lessons from the design of two ADB-funded projects for Mongolia which aim to help support sustainable and equitable tourism. It points to the value of a multi-sector approach and inclusive planning and designs to leverage tourism for sustainable community development, local income generation, conservation, and climate resilience.

Challenges and Opportunities

Despite the growth of ecotourism in Mongolia, accommodating visitors while also protecting natural landscapes is challenging. Strategic approaches that prioritize nature and local communities can address some of the following tourism-related issues in Mongolia, which may be relevant for other tourism contexts in the Asia and Pacific region.

- **Short peak tourism season.** Mongolia's long, cold winters mean short, high-traffic tourism seasons that may leave a heavy footprint, jeopardizing communities, natural resources, and heritage sites.
- **Scaling up infrastructure.** Sanitation, solid waste, and transportation infrastructure and systems require an appropriate scale to accommodate seasonal visitor volumes.

---

11 The International Ecotourism Society. What is Ecotourism? 2015. http://www.ecotourism.org/what-is-ecotourism.
12 World Travel and Tourism Council. 2020. Travel and Tourism Economic Impact 2020 Mongolia. London.
13 United Nations World Tourism Organization. 2021. UNWTO Tourism Data Dashboard.

Integrating Urban Design, Nature, and Heritage for Tourism in a Cold-Climate Country: Preliminary ADB Lessons from Mongolia

Community-centered eco-tourism. ADB's support for Mongolia's growing eco-tourism industry has brought communities to the center of planning, design, and implementation to help spread the benefits of tourism more equitably. (Photo by ADB).

- **Integrating tourism and conservation plans.** Institutional policies, provincial tourism plans, and protected area management plans should be planned in an integrated manner to reinforce each other and bring nature and local communities closer together.
- **Equitable tourism.** Without planning, an increase in visitor numbers to an area may not result in substantial benefits to local communities. This may arise due to several factors, including a lack of local technical skills or financial resources, greater business advantage of external tour operators (access to capital and markets), and the preference of external operators to source external supplies and staff.
- **More comprehensive planning for protected areas.** Management plans for protected areas can integrate planning for natural hazards, climate change and tourism to strengthen visitor satisfaction and safety and conservation values.

The projects provide an opportunity to support Mongolia's growing tourism industry through new income for communities and the protection of nature and heritage, a win-win combination.

— Mark R. Bezuijen, senior environment officer for ADB's East Asia Department

- **COVID-19 pandemic impact.** According to the United Nations World Tourism Organization, the pandemic cost Mongolia an estimated $421 million in tourism revenue. A recent joint study by Mongolia's Tourism Development Center, Association of Tourism Education and Development, the Chamber of Commerce's Tourism Committee, and the Ministry of Environment and Tourism, the country experienced a decrease of 94% in tourist arrivals, a 76% loss in tourism revenues, and a 63% loss in tourism employment between 2020–2021.
- **Government commitment to ecotourism.** Mongolia's development policies commit to establishing Mongolia as a global destination for ecotourism. Sustainable, well-managed tourism is intended to help support Mongolia's recovery from the COVID-19 pandemic. The country is also a member of the Central Asia Regional Economic Cooperation Program (CAREC), which has prioritized tourism for socioeconomic opportunities. Mongolia's vast, globally important protected areas support high biodiversity value and historical and cultural landmarks, and offer a remoteness that is attractive to many adventure tourists. The government intends to expand the country's protected areas from 21% to 30% by 2030 and to scale up conservation, which will require technical and financial support.
- **Post-pandemic recovery efforts.** Starting in 2022, the Government of Mongolia began several initiatives to promote a rapid recovery of the tourism sector and foster ecotourism. The Ministry of Environment and Tourism led a series of stakeholder consultations with industry representatives from the private sector, hospitality, travel and tourism, and protected areas management. These initiatives aim to revise policies, regulations, and standards in the tourism sector with a special focus on ecotourism.

Project-based Solutions

Tourism development is an emerging investment area for ADB in general and specifically for Mongolia. Recognizing an opportunity to support the Government of Mongolia's commitment to tourism, particularly ecotourism, the government and ADB implemented a project funded by the Japan Fund for Prosperous and Resilient Asia and Pacific (JFPR) between 2016 and 2020 to pilot community-based tourism needs in a large national park.[14] Following the lessons and achievements of this project, two lending projects and one new JFPR grant were prepared in 2019 (Phase 1) and 2021 (Phase 2).

"The government sought new tourism opportunities to help support livelihoods, the economy and protection of nature and heritage," said Ongonsar Purev, Senior Environment Officer for ADB's East Asia Department. "The project built on the positive momentum to prioritize ecotourism."

"The projects provide an opportunity to support Mongolia's growing tourism industry through new income for communities and the protection of nature and heritage, a win-win combination," Mark R. Bezuijen explained. "Such efforts are urgently needed to support impoverished rural communities and post-COVID economic recovery, while ensuring that nature and sustainability remain at the forefront of planning."

Innovations
The Phase 1 and Phase 2 projects have been designed to scale up innovations tested under the JFPR grant and introduce new design components.

---

[14] ADB. 2015. Integrated Livelihoods Improvement and Sustainable Tourism in Khuvsgul Lake National Park Project. Manila.

Phase 1
- Mongolia's first loan to focus on tourism and protected areas.
- Preparation of two pilots: an eco-certification program and tourism concession manuals for two national parks. These tools will recognize green-performing tour operators, improve the procedures for issuance and monitoring of tourism licenses, and strengthen procedures and standards for tour camp operations linked with sanitation, solid waste management, local jobs, and promotion of local products and services.

Phase 2
- Application of an international green building design standard to improve energy efficiency for operating two tourism complexes and two tourist streets.[15]
- Support youth entrepreneurs and pilot community-based tourism programs, including microfinancing, training and new market venues to build local tourism initiatives.
- Post-COVID-19 pandemic recovery and resilience measures—new tourism-based jobs combined with a water, sanitation and hygiene program to be implemented by trained youth ambassadors.

Project Locations
The two projects cover rural and urban locations in five provinces of northern and western Mongolia (Figure 11).

Phase 1
Project activities are focused on two large national parks in northern and northeastern Mongolia: Khuvsgul Lake National Park (KLNP) in Khuvsgul Aimag Province and Onon-Balj National Park (OBNP) in Khentii Aimag. Both support iconic tourism values. The KLNP supports Khuvsgul Lake, Mongolia's largest freshwater lake, and the OBNP is the birthplace of Chinggis Khaan (Genghis Khan), Mongolia's most revered historical leader.

The two parks exhibit similar and contrasting features. Both support globally significant biodiversity and small and impoverished rural populations, and both have transboundary river basins with international borders (both with the Russian Federation). Yet each are at different stages of tourism development. The KLNP receives large numbers of visitors, is well connected to urban and rural centers, and already supports many tour camps. For this park, a key challenge is to manage annual visitor numbers. In contrast, the OBNP receives fewer visitors, has few tourism facilities, and limited road access—but a rapid rise in visitor numbers is anticipated due to the pending completion of national road improvements. For this park, the priority is to plan ahead for tourism to help ensure it is managed sustainably.

Iconic tourism value. ADB is supporting Mongolia's Ministry of Environment and Tourism to manage the environmental and social impacts of large numbers of visitors to Khuvsgul Lake National Park. Photo: Khuvsgul Lake National Park Authority.

---

15 Excellence in Design for Greater Efficiencies: https://edgebuildings.com/.

80 Uniquely Urban—Case Studies in Innovative Urban Development

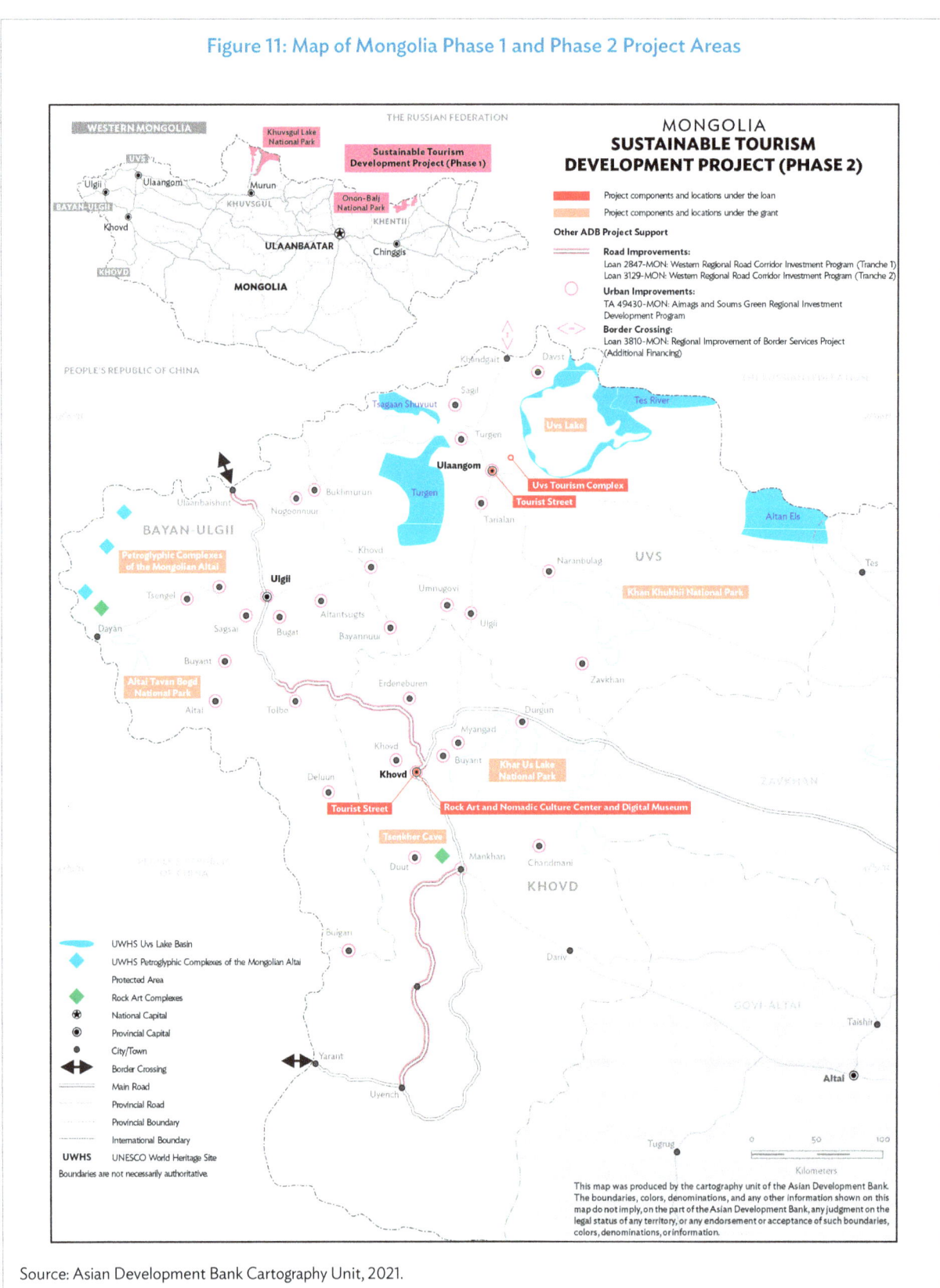

Figure 11: Map of Mongolia Phase 1 and Phase 2 Project Areas

Source: Asian Development Bank Cartography Unit, 2021.

Phase 2

This project focuses on the three asimags (provinces) of Bayan-Ulgii, Khovd, and Uvs in western Mongolia, which share borders with the People's Republic of China and the Russian Federation. Western Mongolia hosts some of the richest and most well-preserved ancient rock art in northern Asia, a rich cultural heritage, and a network of globally important protected areas. Visitor numbers are still relatively small, but before the COVID-19 pandemic were rising rapidly (between 2015 and 2019, visitor numbers increased from about 45,000 to over 141,000).

A Multi-Sector Framework

A multi-sector design framework has been applied for the Phase 1 and Phase 2 projects to balance the needs of development and conservation for sustainable tourism. Both projects are organized around four outputs, with specific design components tailored to local conditions and needs.

Output 1: Inclusive Planning and Capacity for Community-Based Tourism Enhanced

This output aims to strengthen institutional frameworks for tourism planning and to increase the number of local residents benefiting from tourism. Both projects support ecotourism training, developing tourism concession manuals, and certification schemes to strengthen tour operations. The manuals will cover gender development goals, environmental standards, and ways to connect local household enterprises with provincial markets and provide a stable business framework for camp operators and employees. Both projects also support the development of women-led tourism markets and tourist streets. The Phase 2 project will also pilot a tourism development program for communities and micro-, small- and medium-sized enterprises (MSMEs) to include vocational training, a community revolving fund, a youth incubator, and the establishment of 13 community-based organizations.

Output 2: Enabling Infrastructure for Tourism Constructed

This output supports a variety of infrastructure to help manage tourist flows during peak seasons and improve the tourism experience for both tourists and local communities while safeguarding protected areas. Key facilities comprise two tourism complexes, road upgrades, and associated power and water utilities. Under the Phase 1 project, the Chinggis Khaan tourism complex (at the OBNP in Khentii Aimag) will catalyze local tourism development based around the birthplace of Chinggis Khaan. Under the Phase 2 project, the Uvs tourism complex (Uvs Aimag) will catalyze tourism development for western Mongolia. Both complexes will focus on education, heritage, and nature. They will have operational mandates that prioritize local employment and promote community goods and services, working closely with community beneficiaries and MSMEs trained by the projects and in close collaboration with national park agencies. The infrastructure designs apply a best practice green standard for water and energy efficiency, low carbon emissions, and the cost-effective use of local materials.

Output 3: Improved Sanitation and Solid Waste Management

Projections of population and tourism growth undertaken for both projects indicate that in some project locations, without management the volume of solid waste generation may increase by 290% by 2038. This output will support the construction of wastewater treatment plants, landfill sites and recycling procedures, and the installation of gender-sensitive toilet systems in protected areas. The projects will build on design features piloted under a JFPR grant, including operation and maintenance led by trained community teams.

Output 4: Management of Parks, Cultural Heritage Sites, and Protected Areas
This output focuses on the protection of natural and heritage values and improved management of protected areas. Seven national parks and one cultural heritage site (a cave system) will be supported by the projects. Key facilities to be supported include a national park headquarters (at the KLNP), small information centers, ticket collection stations, and improved campsite facilities. Park management plans will be revised to incorporate measures for livelihoods, tourism, and waste control along with updated operational budgets and amendments to park zoning. The revised park management plans will provide central and local government with plans that integrate conservation, tourism, sanitation and livelihoods, and which are aligned with provincial and regional tourism plans.

The Phase 2 project will also support the construction of the first rock art and nomadic culture center in Mongolia. This will include a digital museum with high-quality two- and three-dimensional virtual displays of local rock art. Management of the center and museum will be financed by Operations and maintenance (O&M), entry fees and guided fee-based visits of a national heritage site (Tsenkher Cave).

Notes for Replicating Innovations

The Phase 1 project is in its third year of implementation and the Phase 2 project will begin in 2022. Lessons from each project will be reviewed during implementation. Lessons learned from the design phases of the projects include the following.

> Local communities should be empowered to come up with practical solutions on how to solve problems." said Erdenesaikhan Nyamjav. "So, offer locally tailored solutions aided by research and consultation that can be sustained beyond the project periods.
>
> — Erdenesaikhan Nyamjav, associate social development officer for ADB's Mongolia Resident Mission, East Asia Department.

Gather and Support Local Ideas and Solutions
Mobilizing local support combined with introducing best practices is critical to designing community-based tourism. Project consultations consistently indicated interest, enthusiasm and ideas from local agencies, communities and tour operators to scale up tourism, benefit livelihoods and protect the environment. In particular, women play a major role in community-based tourism in Mongolia and are the primary applicants for micro-loans. Erdenesaikhan Nyamjav, Associate Social Development Officer for ADB's Mongolia Resident Mission, said, "Aided by research and consultation, local communities should be empowered to come up with practical solutions on how to solve problems. So, offer locally tailored solutions that can be sustained beyond the project periods."

Apply a Multi-Sector, and Integrated Approach to Tourism
Tourism development initiatives must be designed to benefit local livelihoods and environmental and heritage protection. To support equitable distribution of tourism benefits, especially local communities, a multi-sector approach is needed to facilitate links between commercial tour operators, communities and government development agencies. "An integrated and inclusive approach brings together tourism, nature, and culture, and can support local livelihoods," said Mark R. Bezuijen, Principal Environment Specialist for ADB.

Each Tourism Site is Unique
Individual tourism sites require customized measures to maximize livelihood benefits, based on factors such as location, visitor flows, environmental and heritage values, and appropriate scales of infrastructure to maintain landscape character.

Sanitation and Waste Management Need Structural and Nonstructural Solutions
Pilot designs and recommendations, which combine structural (wastewater treatment plants and landfills) and nonstructural measures are recommended (water, sanitation, and hygiene campaigns and community-based operations and maintenance arrangements).

Factor In Growth and Climate Projections
Projections of socioeconomic and environmental factors, including population growth, visitor numbers and climate change should be reflected in the choice of infrastructure and design to support resilience, durability, and cost-efficiency. For the Phase 1 project, a detailed climate study to assess climate risks to tourism, nature and park management was prepared; for the Phase 2 project, projections of post-COVID-19 pandemic recovery were prepared to identify the optimal capacity of the planned infrastructure and the economic and financial viability under different recovery scenarios; and for both projects, projections of population growth and pre- and post-pandemic visitor numbers were prepared. To address potential climate impacts, adaptation and mitigation design measures included the avoidance of sites with permafrost (to protect the environment and minimize the risk of building damage from land subsidence); insulated road bases to improve the cold-tolerance of upgraded roads and protect permafrost from vehicle damage, and selection of wastewater treatment plants designed to operate in cold climates.

Best Practice Design Standards
Integrate efficiency into building designs to reduce climate impacts. The Phase 2 project adopted the Excellence in Design for Greater Efficiencies, an international green building design standard, to improve energy efficiency in the feasibility designs. This resulted in avoiding greenhouse emissions. Consideration was needed to balance energy-saving measures and reduced operational costs against increased construction costs.

Follow Women's Lead
Design measures which integrate and promote women's participation and leadership are critical to the success of tourism projects. Gender measures in the Phase 1 and Phase 2 projects minimum targets of 40–50% women's participation in committees, jobs and training established by each project. Both projects will also establish women-led market venues, ensuring that women have safe places to sell local goods and services (developed with the project microfinancing and training) and at least 50–60% of stalls will be allocated to women.

Let women lead. ADB's support for Mongolia's eco-tourism industry includes the establishment of women-led commercial markets, where women sell quality goods they learned to make in project-supported microfinance and livelihood training. At least 50–60% of stalls will be allocated to women.

Learn More

- Watch a project-related video: https://www.adb.org/news/videos/adb-promotes-community-based-ecotourism-mongolia
- Read: Asian Development Blog article: https://blogs.adb.org/blog/blue-skies-and-green-steppe-developing-sustainable-tourism-mongolia
- Project Infographic: https://www.adb.org/news/infographics/sustainable-tourism-development-project-mongolia
- Mongolia: Sustainable Tourism Development Project (Phase 1): https://www.adb.org/projects/50013-001/main
- Mongolia: Sustainable Tourism Development Project (Phase 2): https://www.adb.org/projects/51422-001/main
- Mongolia: Integrated Livelihoods Improvement and Sustainable Tourism in Khuvsgul Lake National Park Project: https://www.adb.org/projects/48216-001/main
- Related case study: Building Climate Building the Climate Change Resilience of Mongolia's Blue Pearl: The Case Study of Khuvsgul Lake National Park: http://dx.doi.org/10.22617/TCS200404-2

UZBEKISTAN

Mortgage Market Sector Development Program

9

The Making of a Market-Based Mortgage Sector

with Peter Marro and Bobir Baisovich Gafurov

Project Name	Mortgage Market Sector Development Program
Project Location	Uzbekistan (Nationwide)
ADB Team	Central and West Asia Public Management, Financial Sector, and Trade Division
Sector	Finance (Subsector: Housing)
Year Approved	2019
Borrower	Government of Uzbekistan
Loan Amount	$200 million
Grant Amount	$800,000
Financial Modalities	$50 million: Sovereign Sector Development Program (SDP) (Policy-Based Loan, Concessional Loan), OCR $150 million: Sovereign SDP – Project (Regular Loan), OCR $800,000: Technical Assistance Grant Fund
Project Scope	Development of a national housing policy and legal and regulatory frameworks for housing; the establishment of a national housing unit within the Ministry of Finance and a wholesale mortgage refinance company
Risk Categorization	Complex
Design Team Leader(s)	Bobir Baisovich Gafurov, Private Sector Development Officer, Peter Marro, Principal Financial Sector Specialist
Executing Agency	Ministry of Finance

Notes: OCR = ordinary capital resources
Source: the Asian Development Bank.

The Development Need

Uzbekistan needs 145,000 urban housing units per year until 2040, far more than what the country has been producing through heavily subsidized government housing programs.[16]

Development Challenges

- Absence of a comprehensive housing finance policy or strategy leading to multiple uncoordinated programs across various ministries and state agencies at deeply subsidized interest rates that were unsustainable for the government.
- A limited number of households were benefiting from the current government's housing subsidies and housing finance programs.
- Non-existent market-based financing for mortgages, refinancing, home renovations, etc., and the dominance of heavily subsidized government housing finance programs would undermine any future development of a more commercially oriented mortgage market.

ADB has provided nearly $1 billion to Uzbekistan for rural housing programs and the government requested ADB's support in replicating its housing projects in urban areas.[17] Peter Marro, principal financial sector specialist, was new to Central and West Asia Department when he was tasked with reviewing ADB's previous investments in the country's housing sector. He worked closely with Bobir Baisovich Gafurov, senior private sector development officer for ADB's Uzbekistan Resident Mission.

During the initial assessment of ADB's previous engagements in the housing sector in Uzbekistan, Marro and Gafurov began advocating for the government to shift its role from the supply side (direct lending and housing construction) to regulation, policy development, building finance market infrastructure, and more efficient assistance for low-income groups. An initial inventory of government housing programs identified more than 20 different types of housing schemes in operation, many of them uncoordinated and hardly funded. The assessment clearly indicated the need to develop and implement a unified national housing finance strategy and identified the need for the establishment of a centralized unit or agency to oversee the sector. The various housing programs were also heavily subsidized ranging from exemptions on import tariffs for construction material, taxes rebates, and discounted interest rates. According to ADB expert estimates, nearly 80% of home construction costs were government subsidies whereas the homebuyers' subsidies accounted for up to 50% of their housing cost, in other words, state-owned engineering companies and construction companies as well as house owners benefitted from excessive financial support from the government.[18]

The government housing finance program also supported rural housing for more upper-middle income households, which may have helped slow migration patterns to urban areas.

---

16 ADB. 2019. Report and Recommendations to the President: Proposed Loans and Technical Assistance Grant Republic of Uzbekistan: Mortgage Market Sector Development Program. Manila
17 The ADB-supported Housing for Integrated Rural Development Program provided a $500 million multi-tranche financing facility in 2011 to fund mortgage loans used to finance the construction of houses in 1,247 massifs (rural housing sites) throughout the country, most of which were near existing communities. In these massifs, 38,461 houses were constructed as single-family houses on 600 square meters. In 2017, ADB provided another $500 million for housing construction through the Affordable Rural Housing Program, which is being implemented from 2017 to 2022.
18 ADB. 2018. Uzbekistan: Mortgage Market Development Program. Housing Policy and Subsidy Component. Manila (Technical Assistance -9479). Prepared by Marja C. Hoek-Smit.

Furthermore, only 8% of all loans provided by the banks were mortgages, compared to over 50% in the U.S., Europe, and other developed markets. Of those 8%, most housing loans were often the heavily discounted government mortgages. As a result, these subsidized mortgages did not allow banks to use these loans as collateral for raising fresh funding because those instruments were not attractive to potential investors. Banks could also not offer commercially priced housing loans because they tended to only have access to short-term deposits (less than 1 year).

Other challenges to developing a mortgage market were the lack of other market institutions such as a wholesale refinancing company, reliable and timely data about the mortgage and housing construction markets, and weak legal and regulatory frameworks to issue mortgage-related financial products.

Project-based Solutions

- Develop a commercial residential mortgage market for future housing development.
- Reform fragmented and costly public housing finance programs and subsidies.

When the project team realized the challenges facing the country and ADB in providing a viable solution, they contacted an eminent global expert in housing finance and policies, Marja Hoek-Smit, the director-founder of the International Housing Finance Program at The Wharton School's Samuel Zell and Robert Lurie Real Estate Center.

At the time of her engagement, the government had only broad housing goals.[19] There were not yet any specific policy objectives for the housing sector or a unified housing finance strategy. Hoek-Smit identified the core objectives of a housing finance strategy for Uzbekistan; the main issues of housing affordability, housing finance, and subsidy issues; and offered short and medium-term policy recommendations to improve the mortgage sector and the current housing finance and subsidy elements of the programs. She pointed the project design in the right direction—toward the innovations required to develop the country's mortgage market. The 2018 study gave ADB something tangible to take to the government. Gafurov said. "We did a lot of explaining to the Ministry of Finance and presented a briefing paper to higher officials. It was important to list all of the issues."

ADB informed the government that if it continued with its present housing finance programs then it would cost the taxpayers about $2 billion over the next 5 years. "Showing the government, the money was an eye opener for them," Marro said. The government was willing to reform the sector, remove market distortions, streamline subsidies, and mobilize the private sector, but the banking and commercial finance markets needed to be supported as well because there was no commercially oriented mortgage market.

---

[19] The government's broad goal for housing was "to expand the role of markets and increase private investment in the housing sector by households and firms, while at the same time expanding the coverage and improving the targeting and efficiency of its social housing programs." Source: Unpublished project consultant's report.

Making mortgages happen. With the maximum loan size being SUM400 million, the ADB-supported mortgage company has supported over 5,000 mortgages to date. Photo: Uzbekistan Mortgage Refinance Company

Innovations and Firsts

To create a commercial mortgage market and reform current public housing finance programs, ADB proposed a mix of financing and technical assistance to:

- Strengthen policy, regulatory, and legal framework for the mortgage finance industry.
- Improve housing strategy and subsidy framework with a new Housing Authority Unit (HAU) within the Ministry of Finance to administer housing finance programs.
- Establish a wholesale mortgage refinance company (the Uzbekistan Mortgage Refinance Company or UMRC) to offer banks long-term, fixed-rate local currency funds to enable more residential mortgage loan products.

What Marro and Gafurov were proposing would be innovative for both ADB and the Government of Uzbekistan. ADB did not have any substantial experience in creating a financial institution like the one proposed. The project would be a learning curve for ADB but also the government.

To support operationalization of UMRC, ADB engaged the he Frankfurt School of Finance & Management and its consulting team of eminent housing finance experts from around the region and the world, mostly active and retired CEOs and board chairpersons of international and national mortgage refinance corporations including from France, Pakistan, Malaysia and Armenia. Together, they designed a plan to establish a new mortgage refinance company as the centerpiece. The team prepared the company's business plan, human resources plan, legal framework, institutional arrangement, internal policies and procedures, list of products and services, and risk management plan. The government believed that the first CEO of the mortgage refinancing company was of utmost importance to building everyone's confidence in this new institution and was directly involved in vetting and hiring the CEO.

Advocating for Innovations

The idea for a new mortgage refinancing company was critical to building a stable residential housing market since the banks did not have access to long-term financing for offering mortgages. The proposed mortgage refinancing company would raise funds in the market, first through development partners and then through commercial sources, especially from the domestic bond markets once they were developed. The commercial banks were interested but initially reluctant to do business with such a new institution. A new financial intermediary institution needed to be properly regulated to gain market confidence. The country had been primarily relying on banks, pawn shops, and microfinance institutions to carry out the role of financial intermediaries. Over time and careful deliberations, the project team and the government agreed to separate ownership and regulation functions to avoid any conflict of interest. Thus, the central bank agreed to regulate the UMRC and the Ministry of Finance became a founding shareholder.

> ADB did not have experience in creating a financial institution like the one we proposed. The project would be a learning curve for staff but also the government.
>
> — Bobir Baisovich Gafurov, Private Sector Development Officer, Uzbekistan Resident Mission

Similar projects from other developing countries had provided useful lessons for the Uzbekistan intervention: ADB looked at case studies from Egypt, Pakistan, Malaysia, France, and Mexico. A detailed demand analysis was also done by carrying out an extensive survey of all banks involved in mortgage finance. Gafurov said they found that the housing gap was not just a financial constraint. "There was also too much government control, right down to the state-owned developers and contractors with little private sector participation," he said.

Meanwhile, the economy was sending strong signals to the government that change was in order. Inflation was rising. The refinance rate at that time could be as high as 14% versus the government rate of 7%. A currency devaluation had addressed the informal currency exchange market, but the project team still believed the government was going to run out of money for its ambitious, yet ineffective housing programs. The government was convinced that it could not afford to *not* develop a commercial housing market as part of its overall strategy for more market-driven development. The government needed and wanted to privatize its commercial banks, so it needed to reform. ADB's mortgage market proposal was an opportunity to contribute to larger economic goals.

A breakthrough came with national political change and within the Ministry of Finance, specifically. Between 2017 and 2018, the government began undertaking critical reforms to liberalize and restructure the economy and undergo fiscal and institutional reforms. A new government issued a presidential decree in support of the proposed reforms and new leadership within the central bank introduced internationally trained, English speaking, and more open-minded managers. "Eventually, with these changes, we got their support," Marro said. In May 2019, the government finally issued the related presidential decree which specifically expressed support for the proposed reforms and the new mortgage refinancing company to develop the country's mortgage market. "That changed everything," Marro said. "From that point on, everyone was engaged. The decree showed that they wanted to change." Even if the change started with a relatively small amount of $200 million it was to be transformational.

Gafurov credits the minister of finance for being committed to resolving the issues between ADB and the government on the mortgage market ideas. "We could have waited years and years for this, but the government determination to reform really helped," he said.

Project Details

Through the Mortgage Market Sector Development Program, ADB is providing a $50 million policy-based loan to support mortgage market reforms that will economize the government's housing subsidy and policy framework and create a conducive environment and infrastructure for market-based mortgage lending. ADB is also providing a $150 million financial intermediation loan to finance the country's new mortgage refinancing company that enables domestic commercial banks to provide residential mortgage and housing improvement loans. To support implementation of the program, ADB is providing a technical assistance grant of $800,000.

The government has established two important entities not just for project implementation but also for long-term mortgage markets. A newly created Housing Assistance Unit under the Ministry of Finance started the housing subsidies reforms. The unit is also developing innovative finance solutions to ensure low-income families benefit from housing programs.

The government also established the Uzbekistan Mortgage Refinancing Company with ADB support and equity investment from the government and commercial banks. The financial institution will provide banks with access to local currency long-term funding. The company will refinance eligible mortgage loans and housing improvement loans issued by participating banks at an interest rate close to market rates.

The project (Box 8) was organized into three outputs that cover policy, regulatory and legal frameworks (output 1), housing finance strategy and subsidy framework (output 2), and a new mortgage refinance company that is functioning with long-term funding (output 3). The policy-based loan financed outputs 1 and 2; the financial intermediation loan financed output 3. The 2018 baseline for many indicators was zero, as none of the actions have been attempted before the project came into effect.

BOX 8

Summary of Intended Results for the Uzbekistan: Mortgage Market Sector Development Program

OUTCOME

Availability of affordable market-based residential mortgage credit increased. By 2024:
- Share of market-based mortgage loans to total mortgage loans of all banks increased to 40%. 2018 baseline: 28%.
- Average initial tenor of market-based mortgage loans lengthened to 10 years (2018 baseline: 7 years).

OUTPUT 1

Policy, regulatory, and legal framework for the mortgage finance industry strengthened. By October 2021:
- A streamlined and consolidated housing finance program announced by the government.
- A pilot-based program of progressive, up-front, targeted government subsidies implemented by. government for housing unit buyers from vulnerable groups, among which at least 30% are women.

OUTPUT 2

Housing finance strategy and subsidy framework strengthened. By October 2019:
- Housing finance strategy adopted.
- Housing Authority Unit (HAU) established.
- Monitoring and information systems for all government housing programs established under the HAU.
- A specialized sex-disaggregated database covering all government subsidy programs as well as Uzbekistan Mortgage Refinancing Company's (UMRC) refinancing program established.

OUTPUT 3

The establishment and operationalization of the mortgage refinancing company supported with long-term funding. By 2019 (except the last three points, by 2023):
- UMRC shareholder subscription agreement signed for the initial capital of at least SUM25 billion.
- Environmental and social management framework adopted.
- Procedures and policies for lending operations, financial management, treasury operations, risk management, and transparent pricing adopted by the UMRC.
- Corporate governance framework acceptable to ADB and internal controls adopted.
- Master refinance agreement which sets out the terms and conditions for accessing the UMRC's refinancing facilities signed by the UMRC and at least three participating financial institutions
- At least 30% of the ADB-funded loan portfolio provided to women.
- At least 5,000 subloans refinanced by the UMRC through ADB's financial intermediation loan.

Source: ADB. 2019. Report and Recommendations to the President: Proposed Loans and Technical Assistance Grant Republic of Uzbekistan: Mortgage Market Sector Development Program. Manila.

Growing families. By strengthening the mortgage market in Uzbekistan, ADB is helping young families secure housing. Photo: Uzbekistan Mortgage Refinance Company.

Concerns for Sustainability and Impact

The startup of the new mortgage refinancing company began in 2020, though initial lending was hampered by the COVID-19 pandemic. Despite the pandemic and lockdowns, approval of UMRC's Regulation by the central bank, formation of initial capital, registration of UMRC with the regulator, development of internal policies and regulations, setting up accounting and other information systems, selection of participating financial institutions took place. Government, UMRC, ADB staff and consultants worked remotely and the company is now well established with two-years in operation and currently employs about 15 people, including an internationally recruited CEO, who is also an Uzbek national. By October 2020, with SUM100 billion from shareholders and access to an ADB Financial Initiative loan, the company began lending and has lent more than $62 million, as of 1 January 2022. With the maximum loan size being SUM400 million, the company has supported over 5,000 mortgages to date.

- In 2019, the government met all policy conditions of the first tranche of the policy loan, which enabled ADB to approve the overall program.
- People increasingly approach banks and get information on mortgages which can also be used for housing repairs and renovations under ADB's program.

- ADB and the government are also working with the state statistics committee on collecting data on the secondary housing markets, such as apartment sales and rental developments which is expected to lead to the establishment of a housing price index.
- The housing market development and the reforms are also providing value and policy support on land use and development, the environment, and energy efficiency.

The same aspects of the project that were designed for stability and growth in the country's housing market—policy, institutional development, market reforms—are not risk free. After all, because the demand is so significant, IFIs cannot keep funding mortgage market expansion without the development of domestic financial markets. Aware of these risks, ADB continues its policy dialogue in Uzbekistan to support the capital market development. The New Financial Markets Development Program was approved in October 2021 and will be implemented through two subprograms from 2021 to 2023.

The Housing Price Index needs to be enhanced to monitor and inform market forces. Since the project got underway, "we are seeing the market take off," Marro said. A housing bubble is possible, if there is unregulated speculation, lack of market information or people buying homes they cannot really afford. Indexes and other mortgage, and housing data can show to the market participants and the government when to slow down mortgage lending or raise interest rates to cool an overheating market. A Housing Price Index is now being published regularly and agencies are sharing data, according to Gafurov.

Notes on Replication

The following recommendations are based on the advice of the project's designers, implementers, and managers. The recommendations are meant to be general practical advice when replicating innovations, though some include specific directives for the project's specific sector or theme.

Consult with world-class experts for designing projects in emerging areas, new markets. Marro said he did not hesitate to contact a global expert to help the government and ADB identify solutions and approaches out of the country's worsening housing problem. Project officers should consider the stakes involved in solving major macro-level social and economic problems when the solutions have a large-scale impact. The most difficult problems will attract the best minds.

Government should drive initiating and ensuring implementation of the reform actions. Detailed research on binding constraints and continuous engagement with all stakeholders is critical for the best ideas to find the right people and time to get a "yes." Uzbekistan's willingness to open up and move to a market economy was a critical factor during the project preparation. The changes and new administration, Marro said, introduced symbiosis for transformational development.

Pay very careful attention to financing structures and mechanisms. When designing projects with complex and multi-layered issues, pay very careful attention to the internal government financing systems and structures. It is paramount to ensure that development partners' financing does not contribute to ineffective public financing schemes.

Consider expanding internal expertise. By establishing the HAU in MOF and the UMRC, the program allowed transfer of international experience and know-how to enhance the internal expertise on the ground. ADB and governments continue to engage with more housing experts and housing finance experts to find solutions that are appropriate for the local socio-economic conditions.

With the right individual and institutional resources, ADB can assist governments in commercial market development and improve access to finance, for instance for subsovereign entities, such municipalities.

Learn More

- Watch a video: Faces of Innovation Video Presentation by Peter Marro.
- Read: https://www.adb.org/projects/51348-001/main

www.ingramcontent.com/pod-product-compliance
Lightning Source LLC
Chambersburg PA
CBHW041247240426
43669CB00028B/3000